Theresa Cotter

Christ Is Risen

♦ ♦ ♦

CELEBRATING LENT, EASTER & PENTECOST

St. Anthony Messenger Press

CINCINNATI, OHIO

Nihil Obstat: Rev. Lawrence Landini, O.F.M.
Rev. Edward J. Gratsch

Imprimi Potest: Rev. John Bok, O.F.M.
Provincial

Imprimatur: +Carl K. Moeddel, V.G.
Archdiocese of Cincinnati
September 26, 1994

The *nihil obstat* and *imprimatur* are a declaration that a book is considered to be free from doctrinal or moral error. It is not implied that those who have granted the *nihil obstat* and *imprimatur* agree with the contents, opinions or statements expressed.

Scripture citations are taken from the *New Revised Standard Version Bible*, ©1989 by the Division of Christian Education of the National Council of the Churches of Christ in the U.S.A., and used by permission.

The quotation from *The Harvard Hillel Sabbath Songbook*, ©1992 by Hillel Foundation of Cambridge, Inc., is used by permission of the publisher, David R. Godine, Publisher, Inc., Boston, Massachusetts.

Quotations from *The Home Planet*, edited by Kevin W. Kelley, ©1988, are used by permission of the publisher, Addison-Wesley Publishing Co., Reading, Massachusetts.

Cover and book design by Julie Lonneman

ISBN 0-86716-200-7

©1994, Theresa Cotter

Published by St. Anthony Messenger Press
Printed in the U.S.A.

*In grateful celebration
and profound awe
of the Holy Spirit—
who soars among us still*

CONTENTS

INTRODUCTION

A divine energy propels us from Ash Wednesday's "Dust thou art!" to Pentecost's "Be filled with the Holy Spirit!" We are on a flooded-with-grace pilgrimage leading us from Lent to Triduum to Eastertide to Pentecost, as we respond to the dynamic summons of the Holy Spirit: Enter into the Paschal Mystery!

We ever celebrate this Paschal Mystery, for it is the foundation of Christianity. During these days, however, we focus on that mystery of divine love; this liturgical time can be referred to as the Paschal Cycle or Season.

This book is intended as a daily companion on our pilgrimage. The meditations begin with Ash Wednesday and continue for each day of that week, of the five full weeks of Lent, of Holy Week and Triduum, of the seven weeks of Eastertide, including Ascension, and conclude with our celebration of Pentecost. Each meditation is complete in itself and independent of the others.

The meditations cover a great diversity of topics, reflecting the complexity and magnitude of Christian life. Each weekday meditation concludes with questions for us to consider, encouraging our assessment of our pilgrimage direction and challenging us to the growth that God envisions for us.

The Sunday meditations ("Listen, Beloved!") are

different. Since our own talking often dominates our prayer, these meditations remind us to listen. I have attempted to write these meditations in a style that encourages turning aside from the surrounding distractions to heed the voice of God within. No questions follow these readings; instead, you are invited to enter into the divine silence. The meditation which serves as an invitation to the season at the beginning of the book ("Address") also follows this pattern.

The Projects section extends beyond "giving up" things for Lent. The lists include many projects for the entire Paschal Season and for Eastertide, as well as nontraditional Lenten observances. The list for families and individuals is followed by a selection of projects suitable for groups and organizations.

And prayers! This book contains many prayers— familiar and traditional ones supplemented with original prayers written especially for the season.

While working on these meditations and prayers I repeatedly encountered within this Paschal Season an integrity, a reassuring wholeness that encompasses all of human existence—life, death and life again. This integrity, this oneness, concerns life of the body and the life of soul and mind and heart; it concerns life of the individual and life of the community. All are fulfilled in the Paschal Mystery.

My prayer is that you, the reader-pilgrim, may find wholeness and fulfillment within this most mysterious and awesome Paschal Season. Shalom!

Address

Listen, Beloved!
Do you know where you are?

Of course you know your address.
You know the location of where you work
and where you spend your day.

You know its locale in the community;
and in the state;
and in the country.

But do you yet realize where you are?

You are on the planet Earth—
one of nine planets whirling around the Sun,
in that part of my creation named the Solar System.

The Sun is but one of a vast spiraling complex—
a complex of 100 billion stars
called by some the "Milky Way Galaxy."

The Milky Way moves within a small cluster
    of galaxies—
half-a-hundred—
your astronomers call the "Local Group."

My Universe is composed of many galaxies
and vast distances of what you call empty space—
but no space is empty

for I am there.

You are on your planet Earth,
in the Solar System,
in the Milky Way Galaxy,
surrounded by
ten thousand billion billion stars
in my Universe.

Yet you—
and all this—
I hold in the palm of my hand.

Lent

A Time of Visioning

We are all called to be saints! That is our ultimate calling, our common mission. We who have been made in the image and likeness of God were created for sainthood. We who have been baptized are destined for sainthood. We who gather in community at the table of the Lord are in process of becoming saints. We who are filled with the Holy Spirit are being guided to sainthood.

No matter what our particular vocational pathway to sainthood, we know that our abilities are not given to us fully developed. We must nurture our talent, practice our skills, seek the support and encouragement of others, continue to grow.

But there is one other thing we must do to attain our goal—whatever that goal may be: We must envision it! No matter what we want to accomplish, what we want to become, what we want to bring into being, nothing will happen unless we first envision it. As the athlete-in-training visualizes herself breaking records, we must visualize ourselves as saints. As the engineer visualizes the perfectly functioning device, we must visualize ourselves as saints. As the still-writing playwright visualizes his play opening on Broadway, we must visualize ourselves as saints. As the student visualizes processing in cap and gown, as the gardener visualizes harvesting the produce, as the cook visualizes a gourmet meal on the table, as the carpenter visualizes the completed house, we must visualize ourselves as saints.

Lent is the season for turning our attention to this call, here and now, in our own time and place. Using the gifts and talents God gave us, amid the challenges and limitations and opportunities surrounding us—we hear and respond to our call to be saints.

CONSIDER:

♦ What does the word *saint* mean to me?

♦ Whom do I know that I consider a saint?

♦ Do I visualize myself as a saint? Why or why not?

♦ How can I respond to my call to sainthood this Paschal Season?

A Time to Touch the Earth

In our sophisticated, high-tech society, we try to conquer Mother Nature—or at least to ignore her. And we do succeed in creating a Mother Nature-less world—except for those instances when her forces produce a cataclysmic event.

Switch-flicking brings us night or day on demand;

tunneling underground and flying above the earth, we manage to touch only what we mortals have produced. Skyscrapers and smog prevent our seeing the stars; walkways and "weather-perfect" environments shield us from the wind and snow and hail and rain and sun. Concrete and tarmac and asphalt and steel and plastic keep us from encountering the dirt of the earth.

But it is touching the earth that reminds us of "dust thou art." It is touching the earth that testifies to the renewing life-and-death-and-resurrection of our cyclic world. It is touching the earth that reminds us of our mortality, our limitations, our lack of control.

And so we must find some earth—and touch it. We must let this soil sift through our hands. Dirt: messy, dirty, dirt; miracle-producing, life-supporting, ever-renewing dirt. We must touch the earth, lest we lose touch with ourselves.

Once we touch the earth, we may feel called to lie down on the earth, resting our body upon the crust of our planet. Closing our eyes, we can feel it turning from day to night to day. We imagine it whirling in space around the sun, ever dying and risnng, from winter to summer to winter again.

We are part of the earth, raised up now, to be lowered once again. We are part of the dirt of the earth, miracle-producing, life-supporting, ever-renewing dirt.

CONSIDER:

♦ What is my favorite season of the year? Why?

♦ How, or when, do I "touch the earth"? When do I
feel connected to the earth? How does it feel?

♦ How do I react to being told I am dust?

A Time of Fasting

Though the Church has greatly modified the
obligations for fasting, this in no way indicates
the unimportance of fasting. Rather, it signifies
the importance of *voluntary* fasting.

There are times when we should fast and abstain
beyond the minimum now required by the Church.
There are times when, for the good of our souls, we
need to cut down or give up, to limit or quit, to practice
self-denial, to offer this sacrifice of fasting to God.

There are also times when we fast in delight, in
anticipation, in joy so great that we seem almost not to
need food! It is this kind of fasting that precedes the
Easter Vigil.

Fasting, an ancient practice found in many
religious traditions, stands in extreme contrast to the
orientation of today's culture. We are surfeited with
persuasive and pervasive temptations to overindulge
in every pleasure. And when we do encounter the
popular pleas for self-discipline, they do not stem from

religious origins but from society's emphasis upon looks, style or social acceptance. Our present obsession with calorie and carbohydrate counts and fat grams can make religious fasting indistinguishable from the "penance" prompted by the latest health fad.

The Church, however, has long advocated fasting, accompanied by almsgiving, as a form of self-denial. And it remains as effective today as it was in the past. Through our awareness of hunger and our need for constant vigilance against breaking the fast, we experience recurring reminders to direct our thoughts to God.

This is the aim of fasting—to remind us of our need for spiritual nourishment. As we experience hunger, we are reminded to pray—pray for ourselves, pray for others, pray to praise God. During Lent, it is especially important that we, as a community and as individuals, include in our prayers those who will soon be joining our community at the Easter Vigil. Fasting is one way we can support the catechumens and candidates on their journey.

CONSIDER:

♦ What has been my experience with fasting and with abstinence?

♦ What is my attitude toward fasting? Do I see a religious element in fasting?

♦ While praying for others is common, have I considered fasting for others? Why or why not?

A Time of the Baptismal Call

The blackened cross on the forehead on Ash Wednesday is our reminder during this season of Lent of our Baptism. We respond to this call by renewing our own baptismal commitments and by participating in the preparation of those to be baptized.

Baptism is a sacrament of the entire Paschal Season. During Lent, our catechumens participate in the Sunday liturgies through the Rite of Election and the Scrutinies, while we, the community, pray and fast for these members-to-be. During Triduum we, as individuals and as community, celebrate our own Baptism by baptizing. During Eastertide we experience the baptismal mission of us all which culminates on Pentecost and our commissioning into the world.

So what is this Baptism that is such an integral part of the Paschal Season? Baptism is:

> the elemental ritual—the first sacrament;
> an initiation into the Body of Christ;
> a sacrament of community;
> a sacrament of unity;
> the community's joyful welcome to new members;
> an event worth celebrating;
> an experience of social justice;
> rejoicing in new life;
> rejoicing in our heritage and traditions;
> a call to faithfulness;

rejoicing in the Communion of Saints;
our renewal as community;
our renewal as individual Christians;
the discovery of new love;
a public celebration of the community of
    believers;
the community's commitment to the nurturing of
    the initiated;
a mystery;
an admission of our humanity;
an invitation to full personhood;
a birthing ritual;
a drowning ritual;
a death-and-transformation ritual;
a recognition of the sacredness of the body;
the beginning of the eucharistic banquet;
an initiation into the community of believers;
an initiation into the death-and-resurrection of
    Christ;
a participation in the priesthood of Christ;
an introduction into the role of prophet;
the beginning of union with Christ as sovereign;
a bonding with Christ, relating to all who are
    baptized;
a commissioning into the missionary ranks of the
    Church;
a sacrament of equality, bestowing a common
    dignity to all;
a bestowal of equality of participation in the
    Church's worship;
a washing away of any claims to preeminence,
    whether of social class, gender, race, ethnic
    background;

a sacrament of God-as-Creator, recalling the
waters of chaos and creation, the flood, the
parting of the Red Sea, the rain and snow that
refresh and nourish the earth;
a sacrament of God-as-Savior, recalling the
profoundly religious event of Christ's baptism
by John in the Jordan River;
a sacrament of God-as-Sustainer, gracing us
with life-giving gifts to help us to fulfillment;
a sacrament of the Trinity;
a joyful occasion to celebrate, to shout and sing:
"Praise be to God! Alleluia!"

CONSIDER:

♦ How do I define Baptism?

♦ How has my definition of Baptism changed over the
years?

♦ How do I regard the non-baptized?

♦ People coming into the Catholic faith who were
baptized in other Christian traditions are not
rebaptized. How do I feel about that?

♦ Do I feel connected to the baptismal preparation of
the new members of my community? If yes, how? If
no, why not?

Silence

Listen, Beloved!

Enter into silence; enter into my silence.

My silence is not the silence
   of those held in captive subordination.
My silence is not the silence
   of those deemed unworthy to speak.
My silence is not the silence
   of those hushed by fear.

My silence is the silence of lovers
   loving beyond words.
My silence is the silence of old friends
   glorying in each other's company.
My silence is the silence of kindred beings
   having no need of words.
My silence is the silence of the repentant
   experiencing forgiveness.
My silence is the silence of the sorrowing
   finding the solace only I can provide.
My silence is the silence of seekers
   discovering at last their heart's delight.

Let go, Beloved, of all that prevents your entering
   into my silence.
Let go of all that hinders your enfolding my
   enriching solitude.

I invite you, my friend, to embrace my silence,
     for only in silence can my Spirit be heard.
Commune with me in my silence.

I AM the Silence.

A Time for Blessing the World

W here is the center of our thoughts and
     prayers and activities?
          For most of us, the center of our lives is
ourselves, with our thoughts and concerns radiating
outward. The boundaries of our lives, the boundaries
of our thoughts and prayers and activities probably
encompass family, neighbors and perhaps
community. But, for many of us, boundaries do exist.
We are concerned about some people, certain
problems, favored sections of the world.

Why are there any boundaries to our thoughts and
prayers and activities? As soon as we draw one
boundary line, we are dividing people into "we" and
"they." Although this may be convenient, it is a
distortion, for "they" really are part of "we." Though
we may differ in the food we eat, the clothes we wear,
the type of shelter we use, such differences are only
the externals of our existence.

We, the people of this earth, are much more alike
than we are different. We all need food, clothing and
shelter to survive. We seek meaning in our existence.
We love and consider ourselves fortunate if we are

loved in return.

And we are all loved by the same God who, even more than we, desires peace and love to reign here on earth. God touches the hearts of all. God opens minds and inspires thought and action.

As our world becomes one global village, it becomes all the more urgent that we turn our attention from the things that divide us and focus on what unites us, for peaceful coexistence cannot come into being on earth unless it first begins in our minds. We are one human race, one family.

So we reach out in our thoughts and bless the world. We bless all the peoples on our planet. We direct our peaceful, loving thoughts and prayers toward all others. We bless the world.

CONSIDER:

♦ Are there boundaries in my world? What are they? Why do I have them? How can I remove them?

♦ How can I begin envisioning the world as one global village?

♦ What can I do to bless the world?

A Time for Cherishing Children

Abraham and Isaac leaving their home to sacrifice to Yahweh. Sarah saying goodbye to them—did she cry?

Abraham and Isaac walking up the mountain. "Hey Dad, we forgot to bring the sacrificial victim!"

Abraham and Isaac, together, building an altar.

Abraham tying Isaac's hands and feet—did Isaac struggle?

Abraham placing his bound son on their altar.

Abraham lifting his arm, holding the knife.

Suddenly the angel comes. "No! God forbids it!" Then what?

Could Abraham and Isaac ever again look at each other without the shadow of that event looming over them?

Did Isaac have nightmares?

Finally, why is this terrifying story included in Scripture?

Before that story became part of written Scripture, it had to survive around the campfires of countless generations. In those days the neighbors of Abraham and Sarah included child sacrifice in their religious rituals. But this story reminded the ancient Hebrews that they were to reject absolutely all child sacrifice. No matter if people nearby observed such practices— they, the descendants of Abraham and Sarah, were to be different! They were to cherish their children; God forbids child sacrifice!

Unfortunately, once again we choose to worship gods who demand child sacrifice: the gods of materialism, greed, career-advancement, convenience, power.

There are millions of children who, although granted life, are deprived of the fulfillment of that life. There are the children who endure various kinds of abuse, suffering at the hands of those who are to protect and care for them. Annually, in the United States, there are nearly two and a half million reported cases of child abuse. The homeless in our country include children and families. Nearly one in every four children under the age of six is growing up in poverty. And an additional number of children suffer from neglect because we adults are too busy.

Surely these frightening statistics paint a picture as horrible as that of Abraham holding the knife over Isaac!

Cherishing our children now—as always—requires both effort and time. Children have the right not only to life, but to a loving and nurturing society. No child is ever sent just to a woman or to a family. Every child is a gift from God to the community, to the nation, to the world. All of us adults have responsibilities to all children, for we provide the environment and society in which our children live. Child sacrifice was forbidden centuries ago; we cannot condone it now.

The anthropologist Margaret Mead once observed:

> Never doubt that a small group of thoughtful, committed citizens can change the world. Indeed it's the only thing that ever has.

CONSIDER:

♦ How do I react to the Abraham and Isaac story?

♦ What can I do to help nurture the young people I know?

♦ What can I do to help create a nurturing environment for children?

♦ What can I do to help cherish children?

A Time for Prayer

One of the most common definitions of prayer is talking to God. There is, however, a problem with that analogy. It is *so easy* to talk! It is easy to pick up a phone, press a single preprogrammed button and converse with someone who may be hundreds or even thousands of miles away.

But prayer is not always that easy. Indeed, this act of self-discipline is more often an easily avoided activity which might more accurately be described as wrestling with God.

For us to pray, we first have to wrestle ourselves away from all the so-called important activities that occupy our attention. Having accomplished that, then God has to wrestle us for our thoughts, which we tend to fill with worries, anxieties and other indications of our lack of faith. As the wrestling continues, often it is only when we are pinned to the ground that we finally acknowledge the divinely-spoken words: "Be still and know that I am God!" (Psalm 46:10a).

Prayer is hard work! To compare prayer to something as physically demanding as wrestling conveys the effort that prayer often entails. Even though we recognize our need for prayer and for the renewal and refreshment that prayer can bring, it remains difficult to do, difficult to work into our daily routine. Like running or jogging or swimming or biking, if praying is done on a regular basis, it becomes easier and we can enjoy more fully the fruits of our endeavors. When we are in good condition physically, much of the strain of daily life becomes easier for us. When we are in good condition prayerfully, much of the strain of daily life becomes easier for us. Only then do we recognize that prayer itself is a blessing.

CONSIDER:

♦ Is my experience of prayer like talking to God, or is it more like wrestling with God?

♦ Do I believe that prayer is necessary to my life? Why or why not?

♦ It has been said that we should not judge our prayer. Do I agree? Why or why not?

A Time of Grace

G race is a personal reminder that we are divinely pursued, embraced, loved. God's grace, lurking everywhere, comes to us wearing many disguises. Often we are most aware of its presence at those moments when we are vividly awakened to the mystery of existence—both our own and God's.

Grace can be an unexpected jolt of joy! It may come to us in the creativity of the cartoonist who makes us laugh, the impetuousness of a kid with a bunch of dandelions, the understanding companionship of a friend, the spontaneity of a bird's song, the affirming intimacy of lovemaking, the beauty of a spectacular sunset, the extemporaneous music that springs forth from within, the reassurance of demonstrated love. Such grace, though abundant and widespread, is offered to us graciously, dependent upon our opening our eyes, our ears, our hearts, our very being, to recognize and receive it in its diverse forms.

But grace is not always pleasant or comforting. Sometimes grace comes as a slap, a blow, upsetting our balance, confusing our mind. It may tear at our flesh, disfiguring, scarring us. It may wound our soul, leaving us bruised and fearful.

Yet such challenging graces never come unaccompanied. No matter the disguise or the terror, companion to the terrible grace is always another grace, a healing, sustaining, uplifting grace. This gentle and sweet grace comforts us touchingly, reminding us we are ever in God's hands.

No matter how or when it comes to us, because grace is from God and of God, it always gives life.

CONSIDER:

♦ How would I define grace?

♦ When have I experienced a joyful grace?

♦ When have I experienced a terrible grace? When did I realize it was indeed a grace?

♦ When have I been aware of being a grace-bringer to others? How did I feel about that?

A Time for Attempting the Absurd

How we treasure our freedoms! How vociferous, even combative, we become when we sense our freedoms are endangered!

Yet we ourselves often freely yield our freedoms. We concede them to society, to our peers, to style-setters, to advertisers and marketing people. We give up control of our lives to outside pressures that determine what is acceptable, what is the norm. And, anxious that we not be considered different, we zealously avoid anything which might be considered weird, or perhaps most importantly, laughable.

That is why we are often embarrassed by the

genuine, by the creative, by the sacred. We fear ever appearing silly or foolish or deviant or religious. Yet happiness and fulfillment and yes, even sanctity, are attained by being true to that inner voice of God calling us to be creative, generous and genuine, loving and, at times, absurd.

God-becoming-human is absurd! Living the gospel is absurd! Eating the Body and Blood of Christ is absurd!

And also, being a foster parent or a missionary is absurd. Being a political activist for nonviolence or opposing the neglect of the marginalized is absurd. Honoring commitments is absurd. Being faithful to ourselves, to others, to God—all these are considered absurd by some.

Yet there are times in our lives when we really should attempt the absurd. Being the person other people expect us to be may not be in harmony with the fulfillment of who we are. That "voice within" may be calling us to do what society has arbitrarily determined to be outside the dictates of convention. The longing that won't go away may be the workings of our inner Christ-light. The Holy Spirit may actually be inspiring us.

If someone near to us attempts the absurd, then so be it! We honor that decision. We wish the person well. We pray for the person and ask his/her prayers in return.

If we are confronted with attempting the absurd, then again, so be it! Only if we respond positively to that absurdity will we be able to say, at some future life-assessing time, "I have no regrets."

CONSIDER:

♦ Have I ever decided to do something that others
consider "absurd"? Why did I do it? How did others
react? How did I feel about it afterward?

♦ Is someone close to me considering "attempting the
absurd"? What is my response? Why?

♦ Is there now an inner longing that I am avoiding?
Why? What are the possible results of my
"absurdity"?

A Time for Loving Enemies

W hen the followers of Christ heard him say,
"Love your enemies," they probably
responded with something like, "Surely that
is a hard saying." Two thousand years later we, the
present-day followers of Christ, agree vigorously.
Loving our enemies is hard!

So we modify the command. Our goal no longer is
to love our enemies; rather, it is to have no enemies.
We change the command, diluting it to an etiquette
book guide:

Be nice to everyone.
Be polite.
Don't hurt anyone's feelings.
Mind your manners.

Certainly there is nothing wrong with being nice or polite. There is nothing wrong with those rules of etiquette. But we must not think that following them is the same as following the command, "Love your enemies."

The message of the gospels is not "Lead a harmless life." Christ's teaching was not simply to avoid evil. Christ's teaching was to do good!

The command to love our enemies assumes that we have enemies. Or, at least, it assumes that we are not afraid of making enemies.

Saints always seem to be getting into trouble! They show us that making enemies is not to be a deterrent to our following the teachings of Christ. And while making enemies is not, of itself, a laudable activity, *not* making enemies is not to be our primary goal.

Christ had enemies—influential, powerful enemies. Christ had enemies whom he knew sought to silence him, yet he said, "Love your enemies." Christ had enemies whom he knew desired his death, yet he said, "Love your enemies." Christ had enemies whom he knew could have him killed, yet again he said, "Love your enemies."

And on the cross, moments away from death, he again said, "Love your enemies." That time, he phrased it, "Forgive them."

CONSIDER:

♦ What does "love your enemies" mean to me?

♦ How do I feel about having enemies?

♦ Does the fear of making enemies keep me from action? How? What is my response?

Mirror

Listen, Beloved!
Look in the mirror, my child.
Do you see in that image what I behold?

Though I perceive everything, there is much I
disregard.
I take notice of neither gender nor stature nor skin
hue.
I take notice of neither curl nor crinkle of hair.
I take notice of neither blemish nor scar, wrinkle
nor age spot.
I take notice of neither excessive poundage nor hair
that is gray.
I measure not physical beauty; neither do I notice
its absence.
I take notice of none of those things by which you
separate yourselves,
for you are all my children.
I glory in all my children.
I glory in your diversity.

Though I see everything about you
I measure only what is within you.
I look beyond what the world sees, and look only at
you.

I see unshed tears.

I see the pain that shadows your smile.
I see dreams that radiate in the darkness
and dreams that are fading.

I see good—
the good of love's sweetness over discord,
the good of unacknowledged courage,
the good of faith's quiet loyalty.

I see in your mirror an image of me.

Do you see in that image what I behold?

A Time for Sensitivity

We human beings constitute an example of extreme contrast. How resilient, strong, determined we are! Marveluus stories attest to the strength and durability of the human spirit. People overcome every sort of barrier, handicap, burden. Individuals survive abuse, deprivation, natural disasters. We are indeed survivors!

Yet, at the very same instant, how frail we are. We are so constituted that we derive much of our feelings about ourselves from those around us. We nourish—or starve—one another. We cherish—or injure—one another. Thus we all carry childhood scars from wounds that people never realized they inflicted—inflicted with that most devastating of weapons, words. A thoughtless word from a harried parent or unthinking relative or overworked teacher—and we are labeled for life.

Our fragility continues to the present: an inconsiderate act of a family member and a relationship is tainted forever; an unkind word from a frustrated coworker and hostility reigns.

Yet how often we ourselves leave our own marks on those who are vulnerable. We do this through the kidding that lasts too long, the nickname that belittles, the "sophisticated" rejoinder, the story with the put-down punch line.

> A gentle tongue is a tree of life. (Proverbs 15:4a)

> The tongue of the wise brings healing.
> (Proverbs 12:18b)

> Do not be called double-tongued,
> and do not lay traps with your tongue.
> (Sirach 5:14)

> Many have fallen by the edge of the sword,
> but not as many as have fallen because of the
> tongue. (Sirach 28:18)

CONSIDER:

♦ What are some of the scars that I carry? How have they affected me?

♦ What kind of humor do I enjoy? Does such humor come at cost to other people?

♦ When have I inflicted wounds with my words? How

do I feel about them now?

A Time of Humility

When we hear the call to be humble, what do we envision? Groveling? "I-am-a-worm" whimpering?

Humility is indeed a virtue, but a virtue often misunderstood and occasionally confused with fear-induced timidity. It even has a long history of being abused: The call to humility has been a handy and effective whip in authoritarian hands to keep others in submission.

Perhaps a helpful guide in understanding humility is to remember two elements of the virtue: honesty and truth.

It is no more humble to deny our gifts than it is to boast about them. It is no more humble to denigrate our talents than it is to vaunt them. It is no more humble to place limitations upon ourselves than it is to consider ourselves beyond limitations.

To seek public office, to seek recognition, to seek publication—these are not of themselves signs of pride. On the contrary, they may reflect the humility that is necessary to go before the public knowing full well the possibility of failure or defeat.

Humility is truthfulness about ourselves, about others, about God. Humility is self-respect and respect for others. Humility is honesty in action and word and thought. Humility is lack of self-consciousness. The humble person is exactly the same in public and in private: genuine, sincere, never wasting energy to put on a show to impress people, never discounting ability or denying developed talents.

Before our Creator we are limited beings with no need of artificially and arbitrarily imposed limitations, sinfulness, lack. Truth itself avoids both arrogant conceit and false humility.

Thus in truth, in humility, we may feel called to prostrate ourselves before our God as beings who do not always respond generously to the love offered to us. In humility, we may feel called to kneel before our Creator as awe-filled beings in the presence of the Almighty. And yes, in humility we may feel called to stand upright before our Creator as having been made in the image of that very same Creator.

Our gifts and talents are reflections of a generous and loving Creator. It is not vain to recognize our talents, for they reflect the glory of the God who gave them to us. But it is in honesty and truth that we recognize that they are gifts from God given for the benefit of all.

CONSIDER:

♦ How would I describe or define humility?

♦ How do I feel when I am around someone who is groveling in "humility"?

♦ How do I feel about recognizing the gifts and talents of others? How do I do this?

♦ How do I feel about acknowledging my own gifts and talents?

A Time of Courage

All growth, whether spiritual, intellectual or emotional, involves extending ourselves beyond the familiar into the unknown—and this takes courage!

We need courage to grow, for growth always implies risk. It takes courage to go beyond the usual, comfortable confines of our lives and risk floundering or embarrassment or criticism or apparent failure. The only true failure, however, is not trying.

We can recall the Parable of the Sower (Matthew 13:1-9), in which the farmer scattered seed and witnessed a variety of results. It requires imagination to think of how the individual seeds might have responded to being sown, to experience the new sensation of being flung upon the earth. Yet such an imaginative exercise is worth attempting.

We know what those seeds do not know—that it is only after the embryo plant leaves the security of its seed-womb and thrusts a shoot forth into an unfamiliar environment that it can come to fruition. Without taking this risk, it dies unfulfilled.

We have a lot in common with the lowly seed, for it is only after we leave the security of our own comfort zone and step forth into the unfamiliar that we ourselves can come to fruition. Extending ourselves and taking risks is a scenario we need to repeat often throughout life.

Irenaeus, a saint of the fourth century, declared that the glory of God is a person fully alive. To be fully alive, to approach our potential, to utilize our God-given gifts: All these require growth—and growth needs courage!

What better focus could we have during Lent than to become fully alive—spiritually, mentally, emotionally; fully alive to our daily work, to our loved ones; fully alive in all our relationships; fully alive to life; fully alive to God. We need courage to be fully alive.

CONSIDER:

♦ Whom would I describe as "fully alive"? Why?

♦ In what areas of my life do I feel "fully alive"?

♦ In what area of my life am I most in need of courage in order to be fully alive? Why?

♦ Deep down, what do I wish I had the courage to do? What prevents me from doing it?

A Time for the Works of Mercy

Lent has traditionally been a time when our attention is directed to performing works of mercy. And that tradition includes two categories of good deeds: the corporal works of mercy and the spiritual works of mercy.

CORPORAL WORKS OF MERCY

To feed the hungry.
To give drink to the thirsty.
To clothe the naked.
To visit the imprisoned.
To shelter the homeless.
To visit the sick.
To bury the dead.

SPIRITUAL WORKS OF MERCY

To admonish the sinner.
To instruct the ignorant.
To counsel the doubtful.
To comfort the sorrowful.
To bear wrongs patiently.
To forgive all injuries.
To pray for the living and the dead.

During medieval times these works of mercy were popular themes for art, with the saint-hero portrayed performing his/her merciful deeds.

Since the needy are with us still, Lent remains a good time to focus on the works of mercy. And if a news-photographer were to record the deeds of a modern saint-in-the-making, he or she would include many scenes similar to those artistic representations of the past.

But there would also be distinct changes, for today we have a broader interpretation of the works of mercy.

"To give drink to the thirsty" could mean working to clean up polluted streams so that future generations would have drinkable water.

"To instruct the ignorant" might mean serving on the school board or working to combat adult illiteracy or picketing for an end to violence in the schools.

"To shelter the homeless" might mean being involved in Habitat for Humanity or helping establish a halfway home for the chemically dependent or for former prisoners, or supporting a neighborhood residential home for the retarded or mentally ill or people with AIDS.

"To comfort the sorrowful" might mean studying and promoting nonviolence or joining MADD (Mothers Against Drunk Driving).

Today the works of mercy may lead us into politics or volunteering with the handicapped or writing letters or protesting business practices or organizing a committee or leading a prayer group. Whatever the particular action the works of mercy remain ways of heeding the gospel's command.

CONSIDER:

♦ How do I interpret and put into action the works of mercy today?

- What new interpretations might I add to the usual list of works of mercy?

- What do I see as the most serious need in my community? How can I help fulfill that need?

A Time of Anticipating Triduum

We know what Christ's followers during his lifetime did not know—how the earthly career of that rabbi would end. With the wisdom of hindsight, we can, throughout Lent, anticipate Triduum.

We look forward to Triduum, to those unique "Three Days" (the translation of the Latin term *Triduum*) that comprise both the center and the high point of the entire liturgical year. In keeping with the Jewish tradition of beginning the *day* at sundown, our *three days* begins with the Last Supper. All the many happenings from Holy Thursday through Easter Sunday form *one* event: the passion-death-resurrection of Christ, the Paschal Mystery.

Our observance of Lent prepares us to participate fully in Triduum. Our participation in the marvelous liturgies of Holy Thursday and Good Friday, our vicarious waiting by the tomb throughout the day of Holy Saturday—all these ready us for our celebration of the Resurrection at the Easter Vigil.

And so now, in the midst of Lent, we anticipate

Triduum. We look forward to Holy Thursday's radical intimacy, which emphasizes the sacredness of family and of community. We know that ahead is the horror of Good Friday, which includes all the pain and disappointment that are part of the human condition. Finally, we know there will be the terrible aloneness of Saturday's tomb-time.

After all this—and only after all this—will we be able to celebrate the Resurrection.

CONSIDER:

♦ What significant family events—weddings, funerals, reunions and the like—have I participated in from the planning stage until the final stage? How did that differ from attending only the main celebration?

♦ How does celebrating Triduum differ from celebrating just Easter Sunday?

♦ How do I regard the celebration of Triduum?

♦ How do I plan to celebrate Triduum?

A Time of Joy

One of the most often repeated directions in Scripture is the concise command "Rejoice!" The virtue of joy has the second listing by Paul in his enumeration of the fruits of the Holy Spirit (see Galatians 5:22). Surely we are meant to be immersed in this virtue.

Joy is a delicate, subtle virtue, fragile as the laughter of children or the blossom of a wildflower. Yet it also possesses the strength of an underground spring that presses its way through earth and around rock to bubble forth, refreshing us and bringing us new life.

Joy is a close kin to humility, a foe of pride and an antidote to despair. Joy is playfulness, happy mischief, an intimacy with nature. And in the canonization process the Church demands proof of the candidate's joy.

If joy is wanting in our lives, we must take care in how we seek this shy and elusive virtue. If we pursue it possessively, it eludes our grasp. If we focus on it, it disappears. But if in our desperation we acknowledge its inaccessibility to us and try instead to bring it to others, we suddenly realize that it has become ours!

Joy, flourishing only in the presence of other virtues, cannot exist alone. Joy is our testament to the presence of an inner core of security in God's care. Joy is our response to the acknowledgment that we are "fearfully and wonderfully made" (see Psalm 139:14). Joy is the echo of God's love in us and a reflection of our faith in that love. Joy comes from our delight in

God and our hope in God's promises.

Our joy in this knowledge leaves no room for pessimism, for God is in charge of the universe. It allows no negative thinking, for God is a positive force in our lives. It allows no deprecating and belittling self-talk, for God is our Creator and we are made in God's image.

Joy can be present in the midst of hardship or absent in the midst of prosperity. Joy comes not from what is around us, but from what is inside us—the firm assurance that God loves us. No matter what the surface confusion and turmoil of our lives, no matter what our age or socioeconomic state, no matter what our need or sorrow, we can be joyous because we view today against the background of eternity with God.

While it is our very nature to be joyous, we may be so distracted in our hectic and myopic world that we can simply forget to be joyful. We can neglect taking time to be grateful for God's gifts. We can bury joy under anxiety, worry. During this intense period of Lent we need to be reminded that being sad or serious is not more "spiritual."

As we remember to be joyful, we experience the renewing and recreative power of this virtue. Joy restores and sustains our capacity for wonder. It brings enthusiasm. It heals and strengthens. These attributes of joy are ours—because God loves us!

CONSIDER:

♦ What makes me feel joyful? Why?

♦ Who makes me feel joyful? How?

♦ Do I ever "forget" to be joyful? If yes, how can I "remember" to be joyful?

♦ How do I bring joy to others? What effect does that have on me?

Pathway

Listen, Beloved!

Bless the path
by which you have come to this place.

Bless the road of life that brought you here,
for you are in the right location.

This is the pathway you are traveling
to meet the good which I have planned
for you.
Proclaim that good!
Congratulate yourself for coming this far.

Your journey is the quest for your own source,
seeking the meaning of your own nature.
You seek me—
and I guide you.

Your path is grace-strewn holy ground
with blessings hidden from view.

Though you do not know what I have planned
    for you,
I tell you now,
my will for you is abundance of every good thing.
Proclaim that good!

My vision of you, my beloved,

is greater than yours.

Bless the path
by which you have come to this place.
Bless the road of life that brought you here.

You are in my light.

A Time of Sacred Places

The places of worship are sacred,
for there we encounter the Divine.
The places of silence are sacred,
for there we encounter ourselves.
The places of conception and birth and death and
burial are sacred,
for all life is of God.
The places of inspiration and dreaming and imagining
are sacred,
for such activity testifies to the presence of the Holy
Spirit.
The places of work and service are sacred,
for there we wash each other's feet.
The places of eating are sacred,
for there do we break bread together.
The places of resting are sacred,
for there we rest as did God after creation.
The places of water are sacred,
for water is life-sustaining and cleansing and
renewing.

The places of land are sacred,
  for land provides us with food and shelter and
    stability and home.
The places of beauty are sacred,
  for beauty enriches the soul and reflects the face of
    God.
There are sacred spaces to remind us that all space is
  sacred.
All of creation is sacred, for it comes from the womb of
  God.

CONSIDER:

♦ Where and what do I consider sacred? Do others
  consider them sacred too?

♦ What makes these places/things sacred? How
  might they be desecrated?

♦ How do I help make places/things sacred?

A Time of Epithets and Epitaphs

How, in a single phrase or sentence, would I
describe myself?
      What one word or phrase conveys the
focus of my life?
   What one word or phrase summarizes my
relationship with others? What one word or phrase

describes my relationship with God?
How might the members of my family describe
me? How might my coworkers refer to me? How might
God speak of me?

What adjectives describing my life could be used in
my obituary? What quote would I choose for my
memorial card? What would I like to have carved on
my tombstone?

How would I like to be remembered by my family?
How would I like to be remembered by my friends?
How would I like to be remembered by God?

CONSIDER:

♦ The above questions.

♦ Are there any answers I would like to change? Why?

♦ What prevents me from making the change?

A Time of Faith

Faith means so much more than a set of dogmas
drawn up by theologians and combined into a
creed! Faith cannot be divorced from reality
or separated from experience, for faith is integral
to each moment of our lives. Faith is what gives us
the courage to face that reality—to greet each day
with at least some confidence and to begin each night

with some serenity.

Faith is the great conqueror—overcoming weariness, obstacles and even reason. Faith, by lessening our anxiety about problems, often enables us to solve them. At other times faith prompts us to request miracles of the God of our belief. Faith is the bedrock that helps us affirm the goodness of God even when all others deny it.

The opposite of faith is not merely the lack of faith, but fear—fear with its attendant worries and panic.

Faith includes our recognition that we are made in God's image, that we are gifted and talented people, and that each one of us has a special and unique role to fulfill in God's plan. Faith leads us to accept that role even if the scenario includes the pain and darkness of Good Friday—for we do believe in the eventual victory and glory of the Resurrection.

These are the faith stories we tell to the new members of the community. In the *Rite of Christian Initiation of Adults,* the preparation of the candidates and catechumens by the community, we deal with our own faith and conversion. We, the community, are the prime agents of catechesis. We teach not only by lecturing on dogmas, but also by telling our faith stories. We teach not by pointing the direction to the candidates, but by walking the journey with them.

The RCIA is not simply a handy way of dealing with new members, for it is necessary to revitalize the Church—*us!* Louis Pasteur, the chemist, stated that a living thing must always be the starting point for the production of more living matter. While he was referring to bacteria and communicable diseases, the truth holds far beyond that focus. Just as human life can come only from the union of the living donations of a man and a woman, so Christian life—a life of faith and love—can come only from the union of an individual and the Christian community.

It is in telling others about our faith that we also learn. It is in listening to the stories of the catechumens and the candidates that we are inspired and renewed in our own faith journey. God is with us!

CONSIDER:

♦ When have I felt my faith to be most strong? Why?

♦ When have I been most aware of my lack of faith? Why?

♦ How do I respond to a lack-of-faith experience?

♦ When have I undergone a Good Friday that led to an Easter Sunday? How did that affect me?

♦ When have I been especially influenced by the faith-stories of others?

A Time of Unifying Our Life

What fractured, fragmented lives we lead! Duties and responsibilities and chosen activities pull us in all directions, while the expectations of others constantly besiege us. As a result of this inner fragmentation, we develop work/professional persona. We have different roles dictated by our family relationships. We have social, public and private personalities. Not content with all these divisions within, we further divide life into secular or religious segments.

The real tragedy of both Christianity and of Catholicism is not that they become involved with the world. Rather, the tragedy is that they are perceived to be apart from the world. The Creator brought forth the universe—including all matter—"and it was good." The Incarnate One has forever lifted up all earthly things. The Holy Spirit is not merely the "Spirit of the Spiritual," but the "Spirit of the World." God is in us and in the universe.

We are now in the midst of this *one* Paschal season that takes us from Ash Wednesday through Lent and Triduum and Ascension to Pentecost. This Paschal Mystery is the cycle of life-death-resurrection which is at the center of our faith. It has one dominant theme: unifying life.

As this Lenten season progresses, we seek this unity in our existence. We seek harmony and balance in what we say and do and believe. We seek beauty and love within ourselves and within the universe. We seek consistency between our inner self and our outward actions. We seek simplicity and wholeness and holiness in all.

CONSIDER:

♦ Is there contradiction and fragmentation in my life? When? What makes me aware of the lack of unity and consistency in my life?

♦ Often it is easier to recognize such lack of unity in others. What do I see around me that could be reflections of my own limitations?

♦ What is one specific thing I can do to help unify my life? What is one specific thing I can do to simplify my life?

A Time of Tree-Planting

Lent is a time of growth, of searching for light, of struggling to find nourishment, of blossoming. We often speak metaphorically of Lent, borrowing terms usually associated with plant life.

Yet what has not been planted can neither grow nor bloom. And so Lent is also a time of planting—and especially, of planting trees. Lent reminds us to take a long-range look at our lives—and what better symbolizes that distant viewpoint than long-lasting and heaven-grasping trees? And so an appropriate

question is: Am I among those who plant trees?
What kind of people plant trees?

Young couples in love,
grandparents,
new homeowners,
optimists,
environmentalists,
teachers of the young,
artists,
romantics,
Scouts and others of similar bent,
humanists,
visionaries,
people of faith,
people of hope.

What kind of people do not plant trees?

People who do not know love,
transients,
the poor,
the short-sighted,
pessimists,
the too-busy,
the self-centered,
the homeless,
people without faith,
people without hope.

♦ Whom do I know who plants trees—literally? Why
do they plant trees?

♦ Am I such a tree-planter? Why or why not?

♦ Whom do I know who plants trees—figuratively?
How do they "plant trees"? Why?

♦ Am I such a tree-planter? Why or why not?

A Time of Anonymity

W hat a word, *anonymity*! We avoid saying it in
public, lest we confuse the placement of the
wandering accents of two similar tongue-
twisting words: *a-non'-y-mous, an'-o-nym'-i-ty.*

Just as the word *anonymity* is not common in our
speech, neither is the concept popular in our society.
When it comes to doing good deeds, we are
encouraged to stand up and be counted for our
altruistic acts. Our employer wants us in the ranks of
those participating in the fund drives. Full
participation, including name, address and telephone
number, is expected of us by charitable organizations,
Church, the community.

The IRS has its own powerful, well-organized
campaign against anonymity. When we make our
contributions of money or items, we ask for proof of

our tax-deductible good deeds.

And of course we do want to set a fine example for our family, the neighbors, our coworkers. For Christianity to be seen in action, we let our doing good be known. Lest our light be hidden under a bushel, we check the spelling of our name on all those lists of active, contributing members of the alumni association, the parish, the community organizations, the charitable causes.

This season of Lent has long been described as a time of prayer, fasting and almsgiving. All our almsgiving, all our well-known good-deed-doing— these are for the welfare of others. For the welfare of our souls, we do good by stealth. We do good in *an'-o-nym'-i-ty.*

CONSIDER:

♦ How do I feel about getting recognized for my good deeds? How do I feel about not getting recognized for my good deeds?

♦ Does getting recognized influence my good-deed-doing? Why or why not?

♦ Do I have any secrets from my family or close friends concerning my good deeds? Why or why not?

Prayers

Listen, Beloved!

Your words betray you.

When you pray,
you send your prayers away—
you send those words and thoughts
away from you,
away from the earth,
out of the biosphere,
out into space—
beyond the moon,
beyond the sun,
beyond Alpha Centauri.

Do you not know
I am everywhere?

Yes, I am in the heavens.
Yes, I am in outer space.
But do not forget,
Beloved,
I am all around you,
and I am in you!

Send your prayers to my image within you.
Send your prayers to my light within you.
Send your prayers to my Spirit within you.

Then I,
and you,
together,
will answer your prayers.

A Time of Seeking

I s God just? Is God really a God of love?
There seems to be abundant evidence that the
answer to both questions is an emphatic "No!"
Many happenings in life apparently contradict the
human concept of a loving and just God.

Yet, somewhere in our lives, we face this evidence,
we confront our hesitation and, in spite of evidence
and our perplexity, we say, "There is a just and loving
God. Though I do not *know*, I will *believe!*"

That is the leap of faith. If everything were
self-evident, there would be no hesitation. If there
were no hesitation, then there would be no need for
faith!

Without the difficulties life raises, we would never
question. Without questions we would not seek
answers. Without seeking we would not learn or grow
or mature.

We might never examine. Without examination we
might never progress. We might never dig in the
darkness and find there the seed-thought that yields
truth.

But most importantly, we could never take a "leap

of faith"—the leap over the chasm of uncertainty.

To argue against knowledge is possible—to weigh fact against conflicting fact. In the face of faith, however, there is no evidence for argument, for faith is not a matter of reason or logic.

It is not just our head-knowledge that leads us to devote our lives to a cause. It is not just a collection of facts that leads us to risk everything. It is our heart-belief that leads us to commitment.

There is an old rabbinic story about Moses and the Israelites and their crossing of the Red Sea. According to this account, Moses extended his arms out over the waters—and nothing happened! There was no parting of the sea. There was no strong wind. No dry land appeared. Nothing happened—until one of the Israelites took the leap of faith and stepped into the water!

God is in the darkness as well as in the light. God is in the question as well as in the faith.

CONSIDER:

♦ When do I seek? Why?

♦ What do I question? Why?

♦ Do I question different things at different times in my life? Why?

♦ How do I respond to my questions? Do I see them as a part of the faith journey?

♦ How do I respond to the questioning of others?

A Time of 'Words in Red'

There are many different ways in which we can read the Gospels. We might decide to follow the lectionary and read the Scriptures chosen for that day. Or we might read each of the Gospels from beginning to end to get a better sense of the particular perspective of each evangelist. Often we search out particular sections of Scripture, prompted by the appeal of poetic passages or the need to find comfort, the desire to read a familiar parable or a favorite story.

Yet another way of experiencing the Gospels is to read only the actual words attributed to Christ. This method does present some obvious drawbacks, since it means omitting both the context of the words and all the intervening narrative. It just may bring some surprises, however.

Some editions of the New Testament are printed in the usual black type except for the words of Christ, which are red. While such an edition may not be our preference to own, it does make it easy to read Christ's words as if they comprised one long monologue.

In reading just the words of Christ we gain a sense of what the Gospel writers remembered as being of utmost importance or most memorable. These are the teachings they did not want to talk about; they wanted them heard as though they had just fallen from Christ's lips.

Doing such a reading usually brings discovery. What is the balance of Christ's teachings? Did Christ really teach what we think he taught? What did Christ say about relationship between God and the individual? About faith? Justice? Love? Institutions and laws? Community? Family? The Holy Spirit? God's very self?

What words did the Word of God enfleshed speak?

CONSIDER:

♦ If I were writing a Gospel account, how would I decide what to put in Christ's own words?

♦ If I could speak to the Gospel writers, what would I like to ask them? Why?

♦ If I could talk to Christ about his life and ministry on earth, what would I want to know? Why?

A Time for Coming Out of Darkness

The rabbi, according to an old story, asked his students a question: "When does night become day?" One by one the students offered their answers.

Is it when I see the first ray of light on the
horizon?
Is it when I can see the path that leads to the
synagogue?
Is it when I can recognize the individual trees in
the forest?
Is it when I can no longer see the stars in the sky?
Is it when I can distinguish the individual sheep
in the flock?
Is it when I can see the bird flying in the sky?

To each of the students' answers, the rabbi shook his
head. To each response the rabbi said, "No, that is not
when night becomes day."

Finally, when the class had become silent, the
rabbi spoke. "Night becomes day when you can
recognize the people around you as your brothers and
your sisters. Until then, no matter how much light
there is in the sky, you are in darkness and it is still
night."

CONSIDER:

♦ What is my reaction to the story?

♦ When did I first "see" all people as my family? What
prompted or enabled the insight?

♦ How can I help others "see"?

♦ There is a difference between seeing all people as

my family and treating them as my brothers and sisters. Where am I in this challenging endeavor?

A Time for Visiting 'Empty' Churches

There is, of course, no such thing as a completely "empty" church.

A Catholic church (or its adoration chapel), is usually filled with the sacramental presence, tabernacle enclosed and attended by the sanctuary lamp's red glow. But even if the sacrament is not present, even if the church appears to be free of all visitors or workers or pray-ers, it is not "empty." And even if it is not "peopled" by carved or stained-glassed saints, it is not "empty."

The church's hallowed walls contain the reverberations of the last liturgy celebrated there—as well as last week's worship and that of last year. The echoes of every prayer prayed and every hymn sung remain. The praise whispered or shouted by all the worshipers who ever gathered there lingers still.

The atoms of the wood and plaster and glass and marble are fused with the *glorias* of Christmas and the *alleluias* of Easter, the *maranathas* of Advent, the *kyrie eleisons* of Lent, the *amens* of our daily belief in God's presence. Everything is impregnated with the praise of God while grace, divinely poured out, still lingers. The place has been sanctified by the faith of those who have gathered there.

Entering an "empty" church is to be surrounded by saints—those formally recognized by the institutional Church, the vast, vast majority of saints who have been recognized only by God, and the last saints in the pews. The space is filled with the faith and energy of all the people who ever prayed there. When we come to worship we are adding our words of praise or petition or doubt or anger to those of our brothers and sisters in Christ who have preceded us—not only those who prayed in that particular "empty" church, but all those who ever prayed! Such is the Communion of Saints—that community, that family to which we on earth belong.

The Communion of Saints is not confined to churches. Rather it is in an "empty" church that often we are most aware of that unseen "cloud of witnesses" (see Hebrews 12:1) to our faith.

Special relationships exist between the living and the dead that defy explanation. That is why we enter an "empty" church in prayerful wonder at both the distance and the closeness between those who live and those who have lived.

Through God's indwelling Spirit we are one with our forefathers and foremothers. As members of the Body of Christ we are related to them all. And those who have preceded us continue to inspire us by the examples of their faith. Our lives add one more chapter to theirs in the story of salvation history, as we recognize the traditions of faith which they handed down to us. We are united, by the common bond of our humanity, to all peoples—to those whose stories have been preserved and to those of the great unknown.

We receive all their gifts in respectful awe. We recognize our responsibilities to those who have gone before, as well as to those who shall follow us in an unbroken chain of belief.

CONSIDER:

♦ What do I experience when I am in an "empty" church?

♦ Where and when have I felt the presence of those who preceded me in faith, such as my relatives and close friends?

♦ Where and when have I felt the presence of my unknown ancestors? Of the faithful people of many generations past?

A Time of Voting Analysis

Throughout Scripture the prophets urge us to look carefully at what we are doing, to examine the reality of our lives. "Listen!" "Repent!" "Hark!" "Look!" "Heed!"

A modern-day prophet might urge us to look at our *voting record*—and remind us that everyday is voting day. During Lent, a time we set aside to examine our actions, it is especially appropriate to scrutinize our daily voting.

Every day is election day! Every item that we purchase is a vote. Every checkout slip represents a marked ballot.

Every store that we patronize, every professional that we hire, every service that we choose is an election choice.

Every stock or bond that we purchase represents an endorsement.

Every job we take, every person we hire indicates our approval.

Every video we buy or rent registers our judgment. Every time we enter a place of entertainment we exercise our option.

Each church that we attend, each charitable cause we support represents a ballot selection.

Every magazine, book, newspaper that we purchase and/or read expresses a voting judgment.

Every mode of transportation we utilize voices our selection.

Every radio program that we choose as background to our activities and waking hours is an expression of our franchise.

Every TV sit-com or news program, talk show or ball game, how-to or drama, current event or exposé, movie or music video—each one that we watch is an expression of our preference.

We are engaged in an ongoing plebiscite each day, for *every* day is election day!

CONSIDER:

♦ How might Christ "vote" today?

♦ How might my votes be evaluated by Third-World
citizens, the homeless and the poor; handicapped
persons, environmentalists and minority members;
the elderly, the young and the unborn?

A Time of Anointing

A eons ago, in a sunny, arid land, oil was an
important element of life. Oil was used for food,
for cooking, for lighting, for protection from
the sun, for medicine, for fragrance, for a balm, for
healing rituals and for cultic rites. Aromatic ointments
were used to indicate those destined for leadership, to
honor those deserving of recognition, to bestow a final
farewell to the deceased.

The word *Messiah* means "anointed," and in Old
Testament times it was through anointing that
Yahweh's Spirit was ritually recognized as abiding in a
person. Later, in the early Christian Church, people
used blessed oil for healing rituals and for the
anointing of the catechumens.

Though life today is much different from scriptural
times, anointing—signing with oil—is not a
meaningless, ancient relic-ritual. We have come to
recognize the sanctity of the body and we
acknowledge that touch—a necessary component of

anointing—is the most fundamental sense. Without human touch, we die. And, without the blessings of others, we wither.

Thus we continue to anoint. Therapists, using oil, massage injured limbs and stressed bodies. Parents anoint their children with baby oil and perfumed liniments and lotions. Those who are dear to us we hug and stroke and caress. Through touching we communicate love and acceptance. Through physical contact with one another we acknowledge the sacredness of each of us, both in soul and in body.

On Holy Thursday, that day overflowing with rich symbolism, prominence is given to the blessed oils. At the special liturgy celebrated by the bishop—the chrism Mass—the three different oils that will be used throughout the year are blessed. Chrism is the oil used at Baptism and Confirmation, and at various other occasions, such as memorials of Baptism. The oil of the sick is used for healing rituals. The oil of catechumens is used in anointing the catechumens and those to be ordained. Anointing continues from antiquity unto today.

CONSIDER:

♦ What does anointing convey to me concerning the body?

♦ Have I witnessed or experienced an "official" anointing? What were my reactions?

♦ Have I witnessed or experienced an "unofficial"

anointing? What were my reactions?

♦ Have I anointed or blessed someone? What were my reactions?

Behold Me

Listen, Beloved!
In all whom you behold, behold me.

I am in all those whose voices are heard on the
airwaves;
I am in all those whose actions are featured in
magazines and newspapers;
I am in all those whose images are on the TV news:

the full-habited cloistered nun praying,
the "crack-baby" crying,
the welfare mother caring for her children,
the two young men holding hands,
the basketball-playing teenagers in wheelchairs,
the bag-lady roaming the streets,
the foreign-speaking dictator,
the saffron-robed Buddhist meditating,
the clapping, swaying, singing, shouting gospel
    choir,
the placard-carrying strikers,
the brain-damaged man doing assembly work,
the rioters lighting the cross in the black family's
    yard,
the weapon-carrying schoolchildren,
the woman dying of AIDS,
the Nazi-uniformed militants marching,
the singing pilgrims.

I am in all those you love, fear, like, hate; I am in all
those you know, know not, understand, *are*. I am in all.

A Time of the Cross

The cross is a symbol of—what?
That simple question has a complex answer,
for the cross has long been with us. It is an
ancient form, certainly predating Christianity. It has
been found in diverse cultures: ancient Indian,
Egyptian, Native American.

To the Jews of Christ's time, the cross, as the death
place of criminals and slaves, symbolized ultimate
degradation and shame. The cross, as a Roman form of
punishment, reminded the Jews of the foreigners'
authority over them.

After Christ's Resurrection, the cross symbolized
to his followers the transformation of their
heartrending despair into the unsurpassable joy of
victory.

Since then, the cross has symbolized the best of
both humanity and religious institutions. It has also
symbolized the worst of humanity and religious
institutions—and everything between these
extremes.

Like all symbols which have survived centuries,
the cross means different things to different people,
for the enduring power of a symbol depends not on an
abstract definition, but on personal experience.

During the past two millennia the cross has

represented unassailable authority, fear, fanaticism, charity, honor, infamy, sadness, mourning, celebration, despair, freedom, domination, compassion, affliction, betrayal, love, hope, liberation. To believers, the cross symbolizes the passion, suffering and death of Christ. It represents atonement, redemption, salvation. It exemplifies hope and resurrection and eternal life. The cross symbolizes the burdens and trials of life. It represents the tearful vale of human existence and the faith that sustains believers throughout this painful journey.

To some, the cross represents the papacy and pageantry and hierarchy, Catholicism and Christianity. To others, the cross is a symbol of superstition and magic, witchcraft and sorcery. The cross is a symbol of anti-Semitism, anti-feminism. The cross has authorized persecutions, pogroms and inquisitions, witch-hunts and heretic burnings. The cross symbolizes the enemy of science, the silencer of inquisitive minds, the destroyer of knowledge.

To some, the cross represents the preservation of knowledge and furtherance of learning. It embodies religious and laypeople committed to education. It represents monasticism and the women and men who have prayed within walls and worked in the world. It represents community and desert hermits and Lourdes pilgrims and TV evangelists.

Crosses of gold, silver, bronze, straw, palm, wood and cloth have led armies: armies of missionaries involved in exploration and exploitation, subjugation and liberation; armies of Teutonic knights and crusaders fighting for the Holy Land; armies of soldiers risking their lives to fight "on God's side."

Crosses are found embroidered on vestments, etched on chalices, scratched on the stones of catacombs and torture chambers and clutched in the death grip of martyrs. Crosses are worn as necklaces, charm bracelets, earrings, key chains, good luck charms. Crosses are located in nursing homes and funeral homes, government buildings, day-care facilities, classrooms. Crosses are hung in meditation rooms and monastic cells and sanctuaries, in courtrooms and birthing rooms, in hospitals and orphanages and leper colonies. Crosses are found on rosaries, coats-of-arms, flags, coffins and tombstones.

There are the initiation crosses signed in the welcoming rite of the RCIA, the hate-conveying crosses set aflame by the Ku Klux Klan, the human crosses of the crucified, the vivid, stunted, beckoning crosses of the Red Cross.

Crosses are signed with water, ashes, oil, ink, pencils, blood; crosses are used in blessings, curses, prayers, oaths, adoration, threats, absolutions, greetings and farewells. The cross symbolizes all of earthly life—and beyond.

CONSIDER:

♦ What various meanings has the cross had for me in the past? Which were the dominant meanings?

♦ What various meanings does the cross have for me now? What has brought about the change in meaning for me?

A Time for Confronting Racism

The discussion on racism came to an immediate reflective halt when one woman asked, "Why isn't racism one of the seven deadly sins?" Why *isn't* racism one of the seven deadly sins? Why doesn't racism rank with those capital sins of pride, greed, lust, anger, gluttony, envy, sloth? Why?

Looking back, we realize that many of our accepted standards of right and wrong were determined long ago when prejudice was an accepted element of life. Regrettably, the history of Christianity is not without blemish! Some of the most outrageous acts of prejudice and bigotry and racism were committed in the names of both Church and God! So, it is no surprise that racism is not included in that old listing.

But we have progressed in our understanding of the command to love one another and of how we are to bring forth the reign of God. Now we can ask the question, "Why isn't racism in our list of the most deadly sins today?" That question can be answered with another question. Is not our racism the result of the presence of those other sinful attitudes? Could it not be that racism is the summation of those seven deadly sins?

Racism manifests our inordinate *pride* in our own race. Racism displays our *greed* for possessions and lands that can be maintained only with a source of cheap labor.

Racism articulates the *lust* that is satisfied only through the availability of the demeaned. Racism expresses the *anger* that needs accessible victims.

Racism survives on the *gluttony* that is satiated only through using and abusing people. Racism feeds off the *envy* that seeks the degradation of others.

Racism is nurtured by the *sloth* that is too overwhelming to counter all the other sins.

CONSIDER:

♦ Have I ever been the victim of discrimination? When? How did I react?

♦ What do I think contributes most to the prevalence of racism?

♦ How can racism be eradicated?

♦ What can I do to eliminate racism?

A Time of Communal Responsibility

Our Christian roots, as described for us in the Hebrew Scriptures, are deep within Israel's social consciousness of faith and worship and sin. This awareness of social responsibility preceded the sense of personal, private responsibility.

For many centuries we Catholics lost sight of these communal elements of our faith; only recently have we re-recognized officially that we are indeed social creatures. As social beings we need to have a communal relationship with God. It is not enough that we pray privately. It is not enough that each of us has an individual relationship with God. Without the social element, that relationship is incomplete.

At the beginning of our eucharistic liturgies we have a few moments to examine our consciences, looking for ways we have failed in our response to God's love for us. In this communal setting, we are to search our hearts—not just for personal and private transgressions, but also for communal sin. How have we *as a community* failed to respond to God's love?

This challenge to the community cannot be met with an examination of conscience that has only a private focus. Unfortunately, just as we lost touch with our need for communal worship, so too we lost our sensitivity to social sin. Thus many of our definitions of sin, our concepts of wrongdoing, our elaborate and convoluted reasonings about both duties and transgressions, are no longer adequate, for they were established during the times when sin was regarded primarily on the personal level.

In earlier times the actions of most individuals were of limited effect. Thus standards of right and wrong were determined when policies and attitudes and actions were dominated by a tiny but powerful minority. Most of humanity concerned themselves with survival—and with the avoidance of personal sin.

Thus we are slow in recognizing our communal responsibilities—and doubly slow in recognizing our communal sinfulness, both of sins committed and of sins of omission.

Yet how much more power do we as individuals have now than in the past! We live in a country where we elect our representatives and our government officials. We vote on constitutional issues. We are literate. We are stockholders and advisory board members. We belong to professional and territorial organizations and to lobbying groups with political power. We are vocal and demanding about our rights. We have ways of determining the kind of country and world we want. Accompanying all of these rights are corresponding responsibilities to the community, the needy, the poor, the marginalized, the world, the future.

At the beginning of our liturgies we must continue to ask ourselves, "How has this faith community failed to bring forth the reign of God?"

There is a saying: No snowflake ever claims responsibility for the avalanche. As rational, social creatures, we cannot claim the snowflake's innocence.

CONSIDER:

♦ When am I most aware of the power of the individual? Why? How does this awareness affect me?

♦ When am I most sensitive to the needs of others? Why? What is my response?

♦ When am I most aware of my part in communal responsibility? How do I carry out this responsibility?

A Time for Youth

L ent is a time of youth and the young in the faith. As our community prepares to welcome its new members at the Easter Vigil, as we individually prepare for the renewal of our baptismal vows, we are reminded of the Baptism of children. Throughout the year Baptisms not only serve to initiate new members into the community, but also to remind us of our responsibilities to those infants and to all children.

We surround the youth in our midst with violence—violence in our society, in the media, on our streets, in our schools. Where are they confronted with gentleness and caring?

We educate our young very early to the physical aspects of sex. Where do they learn of sex as intimately and beautifully and passionately entwined with love and commitment?

We envelop our children with indifference. Where do they encounter responsibility?

We advertise gambling as a way of bettering our lives. Where do our children encounter promotions for education and hard work and perseverance?

We surround our youth with moral laxity. Where do they learn of right and wrong?

We inundate our children with life-styles complicated with wants. Where do they experience a simpler life-style based upon needs?

We beset our youth with paradigms of punishment and vengeance and retaliation. Where do they learn of forgiveness?

We surround our children with a world-in-a-hurry.

Where do they experience a world-with-time-for-the-young?

The task is before us. We must work to make this world worthy of its youth!

CONSIDER:

♦ The above questions.

♦ There is an African saying: "It takes a whole village to raise a child." What do I do for the children in my community? In the world?

♦ What could I be doing for these children?

A Time of Weeping

There is a time to sing—to sing and dance, to clap our hands and praise our God, to shout "Hosanna!" There is a time to wave our branches and carry banners as we process in greeting and gratitude. There is a time to proclaim and prophesy and declare our faith.

And there is a time to weep.

Weeping is our response when we consider the wrong we have done to ourselves: our self-limiting and self-denigrating, our lack of self-love and self-respect, our posturing.

Weeping is our response when we consider the

wrong we have done to our bodies: our failure to appreciate, our self-abuse and self-loathing.

Weeping is our response when we consider the wrong we have done to our family: our pride-filled expectations, our insensitivity, our wall-building, our refusal to love.

Weeping is our response when we consider the wrong we have done to our friends: our self-centeredness, our unresponsiveness, our lack of time, our failure to empower.

Weeping is our response when we consider the wrong we have done to our distant brothers and sisters: our lack of concern, our deliberate exiling, our prejudice, our ignorance and injustice.

Weeping is our response when we consider what we have done to the earth: our self-absorption, our insensitivity to beauty and awe, our inordinate pride of species.

Weeping is our response when we consider what we have done to our God: our limiting definitions, our separations of the family of God, our hatreds and injustices to God's children.

Weeping is the heart-prayer of repentance for sins committed and for good bypassed, for needs of others neglected, for cries for help unheeded, for our complicity with evil, for our deliberate turning away from God's radical, inclusive, unending love.

Some prayers can be expressed only in tears.

CONSIDER:

♦ What does weeping mean to me? A sign of sorrow?

A sign of weakness? Humiliation?

◆ When have I wept—or felt like weeping? Why?

◆ Jesus wept over Jerusalem (see Luke 19:41). What is my response to that report from Scripture?

A Time for Ending Domestic Abuse

How glibly people in liturgy and ministry utilize the poetic phrases and metaphors of the family of God. We sing of one Bread, one Body. We speak of being the Body of Christ. We refer to God as our Creator/Father/Mother.

But do we realize the implications of all this? Do we mean what we say about being one family?

If so, then the violence and degradation and injustice which we allow to exist in this world are all being inflicted upon people who are our brothers and sisters. We, the one human family, belong to a family involved in unloving and hateful relationships. We are a dysfunctional family with a long history of domestic abuse.

We understand the unmeasurable pain that a human parent suffers when a child is violent, unjust, unloving. We sympathize with the human parent whose children are not friends—perhaps are even enemies! In instances like these, our compassion flows to that parent to try to counter that person's grief.

And when our world overflows with violence, injustice, hate—surely this pains the God of love, our Creator/Father/Mother. When members of God's household are sworn enemies we cannot begin to comprehend the grief of our God.

All of us are God's children. All of us, with our skins of various rainbowed hues—of tans and yellows and reds, of lightest browns and deepest blacks—are loved by our Creator/Father/Mother. All of us, with our different languages and life-styles, are loved by our Creator/Father/Mother. All of us, with our different religious rituals and sexual orientations and cultural influences, are loved by our Creator/Father/Mother. All of us, with our different talents and abilities, our pains and joys and fears, our goals and dreams, are loved by our Creator/Father/Mother.

As a parent weeps when a child turns against brother and sister, so God, the Parent of all humanity, weeps for us and for what we do to one another.

CONSIDER:

♦ What does the term "domestic abuse" mean to me?

♦ What does the term "family of God" mean to me?

♦ How do I imagine God feels about what we do to our brothers and sisters?

♦ What can I do to help unite God's family?

Answers

Listen, Beloved!

I know you wonder about suffering in the world.
I hear your questions about pain and grief.
You have the right to ask, Beloved.

For your answer, look to the cross.

When you ask,
"Why does my dear one suffer?"
I answer you from the cross.

When you ask,
"How can this tragedy happen?"
I answer from the cross.

When you ask,
"How can there be peace in the midst of conflict?"
I answer from the cross.

When you ask,
"How should I react to failure?"
I answer from the cross.

When you ask,
"What has God ever done for me?"
I answer from the cross.

When you ask,
"Where is my hope?"

I answer from the cross.

When you ask,
"Where is my God?"
I answer from the cross.

A Time of Passion

The term "Passion of Christ" usually evokes images of Christ's last days, his torture and suffering, his death on the cross.

But the passion of Christ's death came only at the conclusion of the passion of Christ's life. As Christ lived, so did he die.

Christ had a passionate nature! He was the son of a radically loving, flagrantly doting God, a God who not only loves us but is *in love* with us! He is the son of a woman of passionate faith. Mary, Christ's mother, loved God so passionately that she was able to undertake in faith her role in salvation history. Her song, the Magnificat, cannot be labeled the mumblings of a docile and meek female; it is the praise-filled proclamation of a passionate woman!

And so Christ lived, taught, healed with passion. He passionately loved the poor, the marginalized, the suffering. He passionately loved the young and the sick and the grieving and the elderly. He passionately loved Judaism and the Jews and all of humanity. He passionately loved God. The Christ described in the Gospels felt passionately about wrongdoers, about the desecrators of God's house, about oppressors, about those insensitive to the needs of others. Moved by the transformation of passion into compassion, he wept.

We too are called to live passionately—to live and to love passionately, to carry out our roles in salvation history with energy and enthusiasm and ardor. As to how we die—that is in the hands of God.

CONSIDER:

♦ Do I consider Christ a passionate person? Why or why not?

♦ Do I consider Mary a passionate person? Why or why not?

♦ What role should passion have in religion?

♦ When do I experience passion for what I am doing?

♦ How much is passion a factor in my life?

A Time of Myths

Stories are wonderfully effective teaching/ learning devices, for even though a story may not be factually true, it can still convey truths. Many such stories are called "myths."

Unfortunately, the word *myth* has two meanings—

two contradictory and therefore confusing meanings. For instance, a magazine article entitled "Six Myths About the Economy" refers to commonly held beliefs that are actually false. To operate as though these beliefs are true will probably lead to an undesirable result.

But *myth* is also the name given to the stories which convey the great truths. There are family myths, national myths, cultural myths and, of course, religious myths. Such myths, the poetry of faith, contain tremendous energy and power! But it is not the myth itself that is sacred; it is the truth that the myth conveys that is sacred.

All religions have myths. There are the familiar myths of the religions that guide millions and millions of people. There are the uncommon ones of the religions confined to remote tribes and isolated communities. Many of the stories in our Scriptures are myths; the details of the stories may or may not be accurate, but the stories themselves convey the great truths.

Within our myths the basic truths of our humanity and of our faith are presented—birth and death, the purpose of life, the existence of evil and the frailty of humanity, our relationships with ourselves, with each other, with God.

During Lent many of the Scripture readings focus on these basic truths, reminding us to ponder them. We need this season of Lent to clear away the distractions of our sophisticated world. We need this season to remove the time-sponges in our lives and touch the primary elements of human existence. We need this time to look at the "myths"—the truths—of our faith. We need this time to ask ourselves:

> Am I doing what God created me to do? To what
> in my life, in the world, do I say "No!"? And, even
> more important, to what in my life, in the world,
> do I say "Yes!"?

CONSIDER:

♦ The above questions.

♦ What are my favorite family myths? National myths?
Religious myths?

♦ What do I consider to be the strengths of these
myths?

♦ What are the limitations of these myths?

A Time of Saints

We are all called to be saints! That is our main vocation. The writings of the early Church indicate that the first Christians referred to themselves as "saints." Lent is a time set aside for studying, discussing, thinking about saints and sainthood.

The vast, vast majority of saints have never been formally recognized by the institutional Church. That is no concern of ours, for we know that they definitely are recognized by God.

As we renew our acquaintance with the acknowledged saints, it is of great importance to evaluate those saints within the context of their own times—times of famine or plague or plenty, times of political turmoil or religious intolerance or racial hatred, times of discovery and missionary endeavors, even occasional times of peace.

We also see within their lives the tremendous impact of the religious thinking of the day and place. No theology, including Christian theology, ever appeared on earth full-grown. Every theology has developed over time. Our understanding of God, our understanding of our relationship with God, our understanding of what it means to be human—all these are ever changing.

Consequently, our concept of sainthood changes too. Some of the saints of the past indulged in an asceticism consistent with a theology that considered the things of this physical world as insignificant or even evil. There were saints whom today we would describe as being overcome with obsessions. Others appear lacking in common sense. Some seem to have been workaholics, fanatics or possessed by a death-wish.

Yet the lives of these people remain inspiring for us today, here, now. These people illustrate human dedication to belief in the Divine. Their lives shine with their determination to do what they believe is the will of God for them.

While these saints may not inspire us to follow in the footsteps of either their deeds or their life-styles, we can find tremendous inspiration in their dedication to do what they believed God was asking of them. And that, quite simply, is what we are all called to do. That's how we fulfill our calling. That's how we become saints.

CONSIDER:

♦ In the light of Vatican II theology, how would I describe various saintly life-styles?

♦ Whom among my acquaintances do I consider a saint? Why?

♦ What is my response to the statement that I am called to be a saint?

Triduum

HOLY THURSDAY

A Time of Foot-Washing

> After he had washed their feet, had put on his
> robe, and had returned to the table, he said to
> them, "Do you know what I have done to you?
> You call me Teacher and Lord—and you are
> right, for that is what I am. So if I, your Lord and
> Teacher, have washed your feet, you also ought
> to wash one another's feet. For I have set you an
> example, that you also should do as I have done
> to you." (John 13:12-15)

What if we had become a community where worship was foot-washing rather than bread-breaking? What if, when the early Church gathered, they had brought basins and water and soap and towels instead of bread and wine? Would the foot-washing be a practical act or a symbolic act? What might it symbolize?

Who would do the foot-washing? Would everyone present participate in some manner? Would all the members of the community have their feet washed? Would non-members be included?

Would we now have jewel-encrusted gold and silver basins? Would we use hand-embroidered towels of finest linens? Aprons of silk? Velvet covered cushions? Would we use only the purest spring water? Soaps of imported oils? Aromatic ointments? Rare incense?

If we had become a community of foot-washers, what would be our attitude toward bathing? Cleanliness? Our bodies? Would feet be regarded as sacred parts of the body?

Would we have developed an expanded literature of books and essays and hymns and poetry in praise of foot-washing? Would we have innumerable analogies of foot-washing to life and community and relationships? Would we have stained-glass windows portraying feet? And processions with the accoutrements of foot-washing carried with reverence?

Would there be any difference now in the Christian Church or in the world if our central act of worship were foot-washing rather than bread-breaking?

CONSIDER:

♦ The above questions.

♦ How might I be different if our community were foot-washers instead of bread-breakers?

A Time of Integrity

W hy did Christ die? Why did he become death's victim by the excruciating and humiliating criminal penalty of crucifixion? Over the centuries theologians have posited many different answers to that question, debating and philosophizing at length about atonement, redemption, salvation, sin and punishment, and related theological topics.

For today, let us set aside such complicated issues—not because they are unimportant, but rather because of their numerous ramifications and depth they may mask another powerful message in Christ's death.

Let us, for today, think of Christ as simply another human being.

Christ's life—his beliefs and teachings, his words and deeds—were of one whole—undivided and indivisible. Like his garment, which the crucifying soldiers did not separate, his life was woven of a whole cloth, neither mended nor divided.

As Christ taught, so he lived; as Christ preached, so he acted; as Christ lived, so he died. Knowing the logical consequences of his actions, Christ continued to live, to preach and teach and heal and minister, as he believed he was called to do.

Christ, no less human than divine, was a human

being of integrity. Christ was faithful to his Good
News, the gospel; we are called to be no less faithful.

CONSIDER:

◆ If Christ were alive today, for what causes might he
be willing to die?

◆ Is there someone for whom I would be willing to
die? Why or why not?

◆ Is there some cause or right for which I would be
willing to die? Why or why not?

A Time of Hope

It is tomb-time.

We have heard faith preached,
     but now it is tomb-time.

We have heard oh, so much about love,
     but now it is tomb-time.

And now we hope—
     for it is tomb-time.

Hope is the practical, hanging-on-by-our-fingernails virtue that gets us through this day. Hope sustains us through the recurring Good Fridays and tomb-times of our life to the Resurrection. Hope views all of life against the background of eternity; hope measures all things using the standard of God's love. We have hope because we believe in love and life and in the everlasting good, and because we believe in God who is all these. Hope propels us on our journey from pre-Good Friday faith to eternal union with God.

Hope helps us persevere on our journey, not only when the world is against us but also when the world ignores us. Hope bears us up not only when we are considered a worthy foe, but also when in our insignificance and apparent defeat, we aren't even sought as an ally. Hope supports us, not only when we fall flat on our face in failure, but also when our feet are stuck firmly in the mud of mediocrity.

While hope is unquestionably necessary in our battle against ultimate despair, it is also needed to fight against the more common demons of complacency and stagnation. How easy it is to fall into a comfortable rut and watch the world go by! Unfortunately, rut-dwelling gives us a distorted perception of life, cutting us off from understanding, compassion or love.

Hope directs us toward our personal fulfillment on earth and our eternal perfection in heaven. It carries us out of the tomb-imprisonment of our own thoughts and self-imposed limitations into the freedom of our awakened potential. It tells us that it is never too late to learn, to change, to begin again.

CONSIDER:

♦ How do I define or describe hope? What would I consider a "hopeless" situation?

♦ When have I especially felt the need for hope? When have I been most aware of its presence? Its absence?

♦ What gives me hope?

♦ How would I help a friend who is without hope?

Life

Listen, Beloved,
on this day—
the day which I have made—
choose life!

Choose life—
radiant life,
abundant life,
powerful and limitless life.

Choose life!
I do not mean,
dear Beloved,
that you simply not choose death—
for not choosing death
is not equivalent to choosing life.

Choose life—
unselfish life,
radically-lived life,
dynamic life—
life in the consciousness of me!

Embrace aliveness,
wholeheartedly,
creatively,
enthusiastically.

Choose life—
with its awe and mystery and wonderment,
with its pain and turmoil and disappointment,
with its familiarity and surprise,
with its universe-dreamed vision.

Choose life—
love-guided life,
lovingly lived.

Choose life—
life is my legacy to you.

Eastertide

A Celebration of Memories

O ur ears are still ringing with the cries of the Resurrection:

> "Alleluia! Christ is risen!"
> "The stone has been rolled away!"
> "This is the day the Lord has made;
>   let us rejoice and be glad!"
> "Jesus Christ is risen today!"

"Alleluia! Alleluia! Alleluia!" So much has happened! We need time to ponder and discuss the wondrous events of Triduum—the stillpoint of the entire liturgical year.

As we needed the season of Lent to prepare for the celebration which we have just experienced, so now we need time to recall and comprehend the Paschal Mystery. All of us are called to ponder these things— both the neophytes and the long-time Catholics. With the enduring gleam of memory we marvel together at the Incarnation, at Christ's ministry, at the love-gift of the Eucharist, at the unthinkable Good Friday event and Christ's death as a man, and at his Resurrection. We ponder them as a people—the assembly of believers.

All these we celebrated! We gathered as community; we responded to our servant-call with a foot-washing; we prostrated before the cross and prayed for the world; we waited in hope. In the darkness of the church we greeted in song the "Light of Christ!" We proclaimed the Resurrection; we gloried in the age-old stories of salvation history; we baptized and confirmed; we broke bread.

This Eastertide season recapitulates Triduum. The Church calls this time *mystagogia*. It is a time of learning how to celebrate a mystery and at the same time be part of that ongoing mystery!

And while celebrating this life-death-resurrection of Christ we prepare for Pentecost—the completion of the Paschal Cycle. Christ came to bring us the Spirit and we rejoice! To the early Christians, all the days of Eastertide were full of power and majesty; thus are they to be for us.

CONSIDER:

♦ What words of proclamation and joy do I associate with the Resurrection? Why?

♦ What moments or events of Triduum were most memorable for me?

♦ The intensity of Triduum makes it difficult to comprehend its richness. How can I productively use this time of mystagogia?

♦ Is there anything I would like to do differently next Lent/Triduum? Why or why not?

A Celebration of Enthusiasm

The word *enthusiasm* is rather intriguing. It is derived from *en theos*, which means "in the power of God." Enthusiasm comes from without and from within, from those around us and from the Spirit within us. When we are enthusiastic we are quite literally surrounded by the power of God.

Though "enthusiasm" is everywhere, we long-time Christians often become bored or apathetic with our faith. In our desire to appear mature in our relationship with God, we can confuse enthusiasm with immaturity, failing to distinguish between childishness and childlikeness. Having transformed a living, vital element of our life, our *en theos*, into an emotionless intellectual exercise or a set of beliefs with negligible impact upon our words or actions, we can stifle the inner enthusiasm that comes from God.

Those of us who are old in faith need the presence and enthusiasm of the young in faith. We need the stimulation offered by the to-be-baptized. We need the interaction of the recently baptized and confirmed to revitalize our own spiritual seekings. The Vatican II Council recognized the need of the whole community to be involved with the young in faith and shifted the initiation of the new believers from the clergy to the community of believers, in accord with the tradition in the early Church. That's how the RCIA (*Rite of Christian Initiation of Adults*) came into being.

We, the members in the pew, surround the new members of our community with our faith, our piety, our life in God. We, in turn, are revitalized by the

enthusiasm of the young in faith, by those who are
obviously "in the power of God."

CONSIDER:

♦ When was the last time I was "en theos" about
something? How did I respond to the feeling?

♦ What do I consider as advantages/disadvantages of
the community's involvement with the new
members?

♦ How do I feel being around new members of the
community?

A Celebration of Bread

"**A**nd they recognized him at the breaking of
the bread." How? What was unique about
his breaking of the bread? Surely it was not
the bread—the way it smelled or looked or tasted—
common, familiar bread.

"And they recognized him at the breaking of the
bread." Was it the way he held it in his hand—gently—
but not daintily, for his were carpenter's hands.
Reverently—for bread is a symbol of life, and he had
already eaten fully of death. Was it the way he held it
in his hands?

Or was it the way he blessed the bread—bread

already blessed by the Creator's gifts of grain and water; bread blessed by the labor of farmer and miller and baker. Was it the way he blessed the bread?

"And they recognized him at the breaking of the bread." Was it the pain they saw him suffer in the tearing apart of that priceless life-giving substance of body/bread?

"And they recognized him at the breaking of the bread." Was it how he looked at them as he passed the bread? He passed it to all who hungered—not just to those who were worthy, not just to those who belonged, not just to those who believed, but to all who yearned and hungered.

"And they recognized him at the breaking of the bread." Or was it that they, in eating the bread, the bread he had blessed and broken, were transformed? And at last, they could see!

CONSIDER:

♦ What do we see at the breaking of the bread?

♦ What do I see at the breaking of the bread?

♦ What does the breaking of the bread mean to me?

♦ Where besides at Eucharist have I experienced the breaking of the bread?

A Celebration of Jerusalem

I n the souvenir shops in Jerusalem a popular
postcard pictures the world as seen from outer
space with a large arrow pointing to Jerusalem. Of
course, similar postcards are available in many places
throughout the world, but the inference that
Jerusalem is the most important place on the globe is
accurate for some people today just as it most
certainly was in scriptural times.

Jerusalem, mentioned 937 times in the Bible, has
various meanings: Jerusalem is a city in the Holy
Land; Jerusalem is the location of the temple;
Jerusalem is a place in our hearts; Jerusalem is the
center of reality; Jerusalem is the "golden city";
Jerusalem is the Christian community; Jerusalem is
the kingdom of God; Jerusalem is God's presence;
Jerusalem is heaven.

Jerusalem is the dwelling place of the
"Shekhinah"—the light of God, the Holy Spirit.
Jerusalem is the object of the psalmist's longing and
the cause for Christ's weeping. Many events in
Scripture occur "on the way to Jerusalem," that is, on
the way to the place of Christ's death-resurrection.
And every year, at the Passover meal, Jews
throughout the world proclaim, "Next year in
Jerusalem!"

With all the biblical statements of going "up" to
Jerusalem, it might be concluded that the city is
situated on a pinnacle, the highest place in the
surrounding area. Yet, in actuality, such is not the
case: Approaching Jerusalem from the north, the

traveler actually goes down to the city. No matter. In the heart, one always "goes up" to Jerusalem.

Psalm 122 is the pilgrim's greeting to Jerusalem:

I was glad when they said to me,
    "Let us go to the house of the Lord."
Our feet are standing
    within your gates, O Jerusalem.
    Jerusalem—built as a city
    that is bound firmly together.
To it the tribes go up,
    the tribes of the Lord,
as was decreed for Israel,
    to give thanks to the name of the Lord.
For there the thrones for judgment were set up,
    the thrones of the house of David.
    Pray for the peace of Jerusalem:
    "May they prosper who love you.
Peace be within your walls,
    and security within your towers."
For the sake of my relatives and friends
    I will say, "Peace within you."
For the sake of the house of the Lord, our God,
    I will seek your good.

This city, sacred to all the peoples of the Book, is Jewish and Christian and Muslim; this city, whose inhabitants and visitors come from all over the world, is a microcosm of the world. "Shalom, Jerusalem!"

CONSIDER:

♦ What does the city of Jerusalem mean to Jews? To Christians? To Muslims?

- What does Jerusalem mean to me? Why?

- What are some of the reasons that this city, sacred to many people, has been the site of so much violence?

- How can I help bring peace to Jerusalem? To the Holy Land? To the world?

A Celebration of Scripture

There are many ways to read Scripture. We can use sections of Scripture as prayer; we can use it for meditation. We can read it as literature or ersatz history or poetry.

But much of Scripture is story—bare-bones story—with most details omitted. And so, to appreciate fully the stories of Scripture, we acquire knowledge of the cultures and customs of the times, and then we put to work our imagination. Through imagination we enflesh those bare-bones stories until the accounts are peopled with living individuals of three dimensions.

These people of Scripture await our lifting up of them from the inanimate markings on paper and breathing the life of imagination into them so that once again they live; only then do their stories have meaning for us.

These are people like us:

people who leap and dance and sing on this stage
of Scripture;
people who weep and moan and curse and suffer;
people who love and who long for love;
people who believe and doubt, who question and
reject, who wonder and accept;
people who are conceived and who conceive;
people who are born and who give birth;
people who bring life and people who bring death;
people who know joy and lust and anger and
pain, hope and fear and despair;
people who feel;
people who use imagination and intellect;
people who plan and plot, who discover and invent;
people who gaze at the heavens and marvel at
life;
people who dream—dream of wonders, dream of
horrors;
people who seek beauty and harmony and
meaning in life;
people who live.

CONSIDER:

♦ What are the ways in which I usually read Scripture?

♦ Which Scripture characters are most alive to me?
Why?

♦ How do I feel about using imagination when it
comes to working with Scripture? Why?

A Celebration of Affirmation

Louise is an affirmer. Within hours of Louise's departure from a social gathering, the host will receive a phone call communicating Louise's enthusiastic praise of whatever is praiseworthy. Or perhaps it is a meeting that she has just attended—within hours of adjournment off goes a note to the person in charge, complimenting whatever was worthy of compliment.

Watching Louise in the midst of a group is to witness the effect affirmation has on people; after encountering Louise people invariably stand taller or seem more self-confident. Louise is a delight!

But those compliments of Louise's, never feigned or trivial, always go beyond the "pretty dress" or "striking tie" level to focus on the *person*. The compliments recognize the virtues or talents of the individual, or perhaps the generosity of the person in utilizing these gifts for others.

Louise lavishly and generously and sincerely distributes her very important gift—the ability to make others feel good about themselves. Louise's affirmations recognize the need all of us have to be affirmed both in what we are doing and, even more importantly, in who we are.

CONSIDER:

♦ Do I know an affirmer? What is she or he like? What is my response to that person?

- Some people exude a negative attitude toward life and toward others. How do I respond to such people?

- Who around me especially needs affirmation? How can I become more of an affirmer?

A Celebration of Evangelizing

We are the evangelizers of the Church! The work of evangelizing is given not just to the hierarchy or to the religiously-professed, or to the parish staff or to the RCIA program members—but to all of us. We, the People of God, are the evangelizers.

But what is evangelizing?

There are the common images of evangelizing: preaching on street corners; house-by-house canvassing of neighborhoods; handing out biblical tracts; confronting everyone we meet with questions and with *our* answers to those questions.

But other types of evangelizing are also effective. Evangelizing is enthusiastic and compassionate listening to the story of another. Evangelizing is being patient and caring when a coworker undergoes a traumatic experience. Evangelizing is openly and honestly telling our story.

Evangelizing is being open to the gifts of the Holy Spirit—in ourselves and in others. Some of the most effective evangelizers are people who evangelize simply by who they are. We are, after all, human *beings*, not human *doings*.

CONSIDER:

♦ What do I envision when I hear the term *evangelization*?

♦ Have I ever been "evangelized"? How? What was my reaction?

♦ Do I ever experience the sense of being an "evangelist"? When? If I never have, what may be the reasons?

♦ What can I do now to begin to "evangelize"?

SECOND SUNDAY OF EASTER

Wounded

Listen, Beloved!
Listen carefully to the reading of my word.

Did you hear the story of Thomas—
my friend Thomas and his doubtfulness?

Did you hear
how Thomas recognized me?
Do you recall?

It was not by my breaking of the bread;
it was not by the wisdom of my words;
it was not by the force of his intellect;
it was not by the attendance of my angels.

My friend Thomas knew me
by my wounds.

By my woundedness
he recognized me—
the risen Christ.

Look around you now, Beloved,
You too will recognize me—
the Christ—
by my wounds.

Observe the wounded around you—
the poor,

the suffering,
the lonely.
I am in them.
Their wounds are my wounds.

Do you see me?
Or do you still doubt?

Do not mistrust me.
Put your hand in the wounds
and believe!

A Celebration of the Holy Spirit

The Holy Spirit, that shy member of the Trinity,
calls us to mystery and to mystical
wonderment. The Spirit most holy is best
known through progressively unfolding action and
inspiration, and is traditionally recognized as the
bestower of gifts and fruits.
   The Holy Spirit:

> is the hand of God;
> is the continuity of Christianity;
> is necessary for the proclamation of the Word;
> is more radically present than expected;
> works in individuals;
> works in communities;
> is the main actor in the Church's mission;
> is our counselor, the Paraclete;
> is the source of all good;

was present before creation;
is present at Baptism;
mediates the Eucharist;
is the *Ruah* ("breath") of the Hebrew Scriptures;
is the *Shekinah* ("light") of the Hebrew
     Scriptures;
is the Sophia/Wisdom of Scripture, Lady
     Wisdom;
is the Wisdom which preceded creation;
resists labels;
is concerned about the oppressed;
is the source of all that is creative;
is the outpouring presence of the eternal divine
     Love;
gives power and efficacy to the gospel;
is life;
is the feminine face of God;
teaches through experience;
is laughter;
is alive and moving and working;
is anti-rigidity;
brings the freedom that is necessary for love;
is freedom and is the desire for freedom;
is in the struggle for freedom;
is intimately connected with the Word;
is present where there is openness;
is celebrated in the Sacrament of Confirmation;
is the driving force of creation;
is the animating breath of the universe;
is hidden, yet obvious;
is obvious, yet hidden;
is silence;
is the wind;

is light;
is the dispenser of grace;
is surprise—unpredictable, whimsical, surprise;
is the laughter in the midst of struggle and pain;
does not discriminate;
is the breath of music-making;
is unknown, unbounded, unimagined;
most adequately reflects the nature of God;
sparks conversion;
encourages the struggle for liberation;
commissions us to ministry;
is active in the common people;
is the eternal fire;
is the God of the eternal now;
is always present.

As John the Baptist prepared the way for Christ, so Christ prepared the way for the Holy Spirit to enter our awareness and consciousness.

CONSIDER:

♦ Who/what is the Holy Spirit to me? How do I usually envision the Spirit?

♦ When am I most aware of the Holy Spirit? Why?

♦ Where, in my relationship to God, are dancing and singing and laughter and surprise?

♦ What part does the Holy Spirit take in my relationship to God? Why?

A Celebration of Community

Freedom is one of the dominant themes in Scripture.

The God who created us graced us with free wills. The Paschal Mystery frees us from the fear of death; the Exodus experience is considered the main event of the Hebrew Scriptures.

But we confuse freedom with individualism, which our culture has idealized. Rugged, fiercely independent individualism has become an obsession, offering the goal of each individual becoming a species unto oneself.

Such commitment to individualism, however, comes at great cost as we sacrifice our need for community.

It has been speculated that the real reason the Israelites wandered for forty years in the desert was that they needed the shared experiences of that lengthy time to be transformed from a bunch of former slaves into the community of the chosen people. Without undergoing forty years together, they would not have learned the necessary interdependence and mutuality.

Communities grow from the bottom up. Communities cultivate and nurture *being* more rather than *having* more. Communities share not just goods, but also public action—such as worship, which is carried out in common. Communities are experiences of the Holy Spirit, which means they are active, freeing, life-giving experiences.

Because communities are experiences of the Holy

Spirit, there is freedom within community, since freedom is one of the most obvious evidences of the active presence of the Spirit. Freedom and interdependence exist in community, nurturing the potential of the individuals belonging to the community and thus giving life to the community itself. The agape love of community is regarded by Paul as the greatest fruit of the Holy Spirit. It is this agape, this solidarity, this bond of mutual commitment, which builds community—and community in turn produces Church!

CONSIDER:

♦ How would I describe or define community?

♦ It has been said "Without community, whose feet would we wash?" What is my response?

♦ When members of the Church community do not attend liturgy or do not participate, the community suffers. What is my response?

♦ The Navajo people describe a person who does something dishonest or unworthy as acting as though that person had no relatives—as though not part of the community. What is my response?

A Celebration of the Flame

Is it due to our collective genetic memory that we are so fascinated with the flame?

The flame has long been considered symbolic by many peoples. Perhaps it has to do with the lifelike movement of the flame, or its power to mesmerize, or its mighty usefulness/destructiveness, or that it is always pointed upward in the direction of the heavens, the traditional residence of superhuman beings. Whatever the reason, the flame is often used as a "living" memorial of the dead, as a focal point of meditation, as a symbol of the divine or eternal.

An awe-inspiring use of the flame's symbolism is in the Children's Memorial at Yad Vashem, the Holocaust Memorial in Jerusalem. This testament to a nation's grief consists of various museum and archive buildings incorporating many impressive works of art, all set in a parklike environment.

The Children's Memorial commemorates the one and a half million children slaughtered during the Holocaust. The intent of the design is to communicate some realization of that vast number of living beings who were prevented from ever reaching adulthood, for how can a person comprehend the extinguishing of one and a half million lives?

The curving path to the Children's Memorial is marked with long cylindrical lamps and natural stone in a garden setting. Portraits of Jewish children of different nationalities line the entranceway. The visitor, guided by a handrail, enters a gradually darkening area, while over the background of Jewish music recorded voices recite the names and ages of martyred children. After one more turn the visitor is in a large dark room lighted only by the flickering reflections of a seemingly countless number of candle flames—everywhere! Only five candles are actually burning, yet this startling environment is achieved by the careful positioning of reflective surfaces.

Overcome by the cumulative effect of the flames, the music, the litany of murdered children, the visitor stands silent. One and a half million children! Visitors to the Children's Memorial often are in tears upon leaving the stark simplicity of the building.

CONSIDER:

♦ What does the flame symbolize for me? Where have I encountered symbolic uses of the flame? How effective were they?

♦ At the Easter Vigil, the Paschal Candle is greeted with the sung phrase, "Light of Christ." What does the Easter candle symbolize for me?

♦ If there had been more Christians truly reflecting the "Light of Christ," would the Holocaust have taken place? Why is that my answer?

A Celebration of the Indwelling Presence

The Holy Spirit is *not* a gas station attendant! Back in antiquity, ages before such things as automobiles were ever envisioned, the tradition was established that prayers to the Holy Spirit begin with the words: "Come, Holy Spirit! Fill us with ...."

The result of all these prayer-beginnings is that we tend to visualize the Holy Spirit as a Trinitarian gasoline dispenser at the supreme-octane filling station. Perhaps prompted by the "coming" of the Holy Spirit on Pentecost, we envision the Holy Spirit working from above, occasionally touching us like a fairy godmother using her wand, dispensing into us whatever virtue is needed at the moment.

There is, of course, nothing wrong with that image, as long as we realize that it—like all images and metaphors and icons of God—illustrates only a partial aspect of the Infinite. There is, however, a danger inherent with that image. The danger is that we become so accustomed to thinking of the Holy Spirit as outside or above or away that we forget that the Holy Spirit is *within* and *here*.

In the Nicene Creed we affirm that "We believe in the Holy Spirit, the Lord, the giver of life...." The Holy Spirit, as the giver and sustainer of life, is within us and within all of creation. If the Holy Spirit were not present, we and the rest of the universe would simply cease to exist.

We need the Spirit for our existence; we need the Spirit to reach the fullness of humanity that lies within our potential. And so, while we rightly pray to the Holy Spirit, our need for help is often to be saved from ourselves.

We carry within us many talents and virtues and strengths. We are just beginning to realize the potential of humanity! We can, however, bury our talents under neglect and laziness; we can hide our virtues behind false humility and culture-based standards of behavior; we can allow our strengths to atrophy through disuse.

And so we do need the Holy Spirit! We need the Holy Spirit—not necessarily as a gas station attendant to "fill 'er up!" but to help us to fulfill our potential. There are other images we might consider: the Holy Spirit as the keeper of the keys who helps us unlock our talents; the Holy Spirit as a treasure finder who helps us locate our God-given abilities; the Holy Spirit as a heavy-machinery operator to help us remove the debris we ourselves have heaped upon our assets.

Perhaps we might try beginning our prayers to the Holy Spirit thus:

"Come forth, Holy Spirit! Free within us..."; or "Indwelling Spirit most holy, let your light shine within us!"

CONSIDER:

♦ How do I envision the Holy Spirit?

♦ How do I envision the Holy Spirit's help?

♦ Where is the Holy Spirit in my life? Do I pray to the Holy Spirit? What words do I use?

A Celebration of Brown-Bag Lunches

The multitude ate and were filled. There was abundance; there was surplus. All that food came from the breaking of the bread and the blessing of the fish. Christ took the bread and blessed it—and fed the multitudes.

Obviously the Gospel writers considered this an important event, for it is the only one of Christ's miracles recounted by all four evangelists.

Christ took bread. Now Our Lord could have done an *abracadabra* and suddenly there would have been bread for all. But he didn't. Christ always began his miracles with the fruits of human efforts, our efforts. Where did the bread come from? Scripture tells us simply "a young boy" had some loaves and fish.

A "young boy" usually does not plan ahead. So let's imagine a scene that might have preceded the events in our Gospel reading. Our friend—let's say his name is Samuel—has just talked his parents into letting him spend the day listening to the itinerant preacher in the vicinity.

"You just might learn something!" his father says.

But as Samuel is going out the door, his mother hurries after him. "Here, take something to eat—I know you'll get hungry. And mind your manners!" (Probably no mother, beginning with Eve, ever sent a child forth without the injunction, "Mind your manners!")

Carrying his brown-bag lunch, our Samuel takes off to spend the day listening to the rabbi called Jesus. And mind his manners Samuel did. He did not eat his lunch in the presence of all those other hungry people. And, when asked to donate the contents of that little brown bag, he gave it to the disciples. And a miracle occurred! We can't help but smile as we imagine the scene when our Samuel returns home. "Mom! Remember that lunch you packed for me? You'll never believe what happened to it!"

We do not perform miracles. But because we do our duty, because we do those thousand and one little tasks that seem so trivial and mundane, miracles occur.

And so we are faithful. We persevere in all those seemingly insignificant things involving family and friends and job and community. We care for kids and customers, patients and students, yards and homes; we fix meals and cars and wounds; we speak to answering machines and fill out forms and make our quotas; we attend classes and seminars and meetings and church services. It is through these routine tasks that we make available to God, day after day, our loaves of bread. We perform our duties; we are faithful. And sometimes God takes one of those loaves of bread, and blesses it and breaks it, and multitudes are fed.

CONSIDER:

♦ When do the oh-so-daily tasks of life seem
  meaningless to me?

♦ When am I able to see in the mundane tasks of daily
  living the seeds of miracles?

♦ What makes the difference in how I view my life?

♦ How do I handle "being in a rut"?

A Celebration of Church

M any of the Eastertide Scripture readings are
from the Acts of the Apostles, Luke's
account of the early Church. Here are the
stories of those first pioneer Christians—the newly-
converted Jews and Gentiles; here are the struggles of
the first Christians to discover and define who they
were before the term *Christian* was used. All the new
members of this religion were involved in the
evangelization and catechizing of the even-newer
members, for that was the mission of everyone in the
early Church.

But what was this "early Church"? There were no
chapels or buildings or temples carrying the
designation *church*; there were no dioceses or
seminaries or chanceries; there were no synods or
councils or parish boards. There were no stained-glass

windows or statues or tabernacles or pipe organs; there were no guitars or amplification systems or worship-aid handouts or church bulletins. There were no lectionaries or sacramentaries or breviaries. There were no religious education programs or building fund drives or parish missions. There was no canon law; neither was there a catechism. There wasn't even a book to tell them what to do when they gathered.

But there was a Church! The "early Church" meant the people; the "present Church" means the people. Because the Church *is* the people, it is always young/elderly, sinful/saintly, birthing/dying, hating/loving, doubting/believing, ever-new/ever-old, forgetting/remembering, wrong/right, fearful/courageous, ever-constant/ever-changing. *People* were and are and ever shall be the Church.

CONSIDER:

♦ *We* are the Church!

♦ We *are* the Church!

♦ We are *the* Church!

♦ We are the *Church*!

Desire

Listen, Beloved!

What more do you desire?

Out of love I created you;
the spark of the divine is within you;
it is my Spirit that sustains you.
What more do you desire?

In you, Beloved, I have placed my love;
in you I have invested energy and concern.
What more do you desire?

You and I are united in humanity—
I became one of you;
I walked on your earth;
I shared tears and laughter and human life.
What more do you desire?

Nor have I left you alone.
I remain with you still—
in bread and wine,
in word,
in all people—
I surround you!
What more do you desire?

I am in all those close to you:
those who know your name,

those who recognize your face.
I am in those you have yet to meet.
What more do you desire?

And I am in you!
My Spirit resides in you,
lovingly, everlastingly.
What more do you desire?

A Celebration of Gratitude

As we ponder the mysteries of Triduum and of God's incomprehensible love, we eventually realize with renewed vigor our gratitude to God. We are grateful, not only for the spectacular and miraculous, but also for everyday blessings and miracles of life taken for granted.

We can express that gratitude in words and thoughts, acknowledging God as the source of all good. But gratitude is even more eloquently expressed in using God's gifts for others, spreading God's radical and inclusive love through our own generosity.

Unlike the more heroic virtues, gratitude does not require personal sacrifice in battle or unselfish commitment as a missionary to a remote island. Since gratitude, like joy, can bring happiness and satisfaction to both giver and receiver—and with relatively little effort—we may minimize its importance, relegating it to social convention rather than the virtuous life.

Yet gratitude is necessary for community, for it reminds us of our interdependence. It acknowledges the many ways that we as individuals and as members of society have benefited from the generosity of those who preceded us. Our social, political and religious structures, our schools and churches and parks were built and supported by unselfish, far-thinking people. And our day-to-day experiences illustrate the cooperation we need to function as community. In thankful response to all these people, we too must be generous—both to those here now and to those who will follow.

Expressing our thankfulness not only brings us pleasure, but also revitalizes and renews the commitment of others to their jobs, professions and duties, or to Christian charity. Only God knows how many dedicated people have despaired of their own usefulness or vocation because of a lack of gratitude from those they served.

Gratitude is also a stabilizing virtue, assisting us in keeping our own priorities in balance. And a heart filled with gratitude has no room for that most insidious of vices—pride—for the recognition of our mutual dependence prevents self-centeredness. As we concentrate on this virtue of gratitude and testify to its presence in our lives by our own generosity, it is consoling to remember that we can never outgive God.

CONSIDER:

- ♦ What are the gifts from God for which I am most grateful?

- ♦ How do I express my gratitude to God? To family members? To teachers and others from my youth? To the members of my community? To the world?

- ♦ How do I encourage gratitude in others?

A Celebration of Presence

How annoying! We are talking to a friend—and suddenly we know he is not listening to us. Or perhaps we are visiting a neighbor—and at some moment we know she has left us in spirit and her thoughts are elsewhere. We do feel annoyed, perhaps insulted.

Such experiences are common, for our fragmented, disjointed lives slowly beat us into fragmented, disjointed people. While our body is engaged in one activity, our mind is facing other challenges while our spirits and hearts seek yet other escapes. We become less than the sum of our parts, for each is lessened by the absence of the others.

Rarely are we truly present to others. But when our senses and attributes are united, when the confluence of hands and soul and spirit and heart occurs, then we are able to offer to one another our presence.

Only then can we listen with full consciousness to what another is saying; only then are we receptive to the words and emotions and thoughts conveyed. In this state of presence we do not begin to speak until we have first entered into silence, knowing we need time to consider our response.

In this state of presence we are aware of the world around us. We are aware of the creations of God and of the creations of humanity; we are aware of being part of all. We are conscious of this day, this time, this opportunity, these people, this life.

And we are conscious of God's presence and of God's consciousness of us, for without that we would be nothing. Literally, nothing! It is this total presence that describes God's presence to us. God always gifts us with total presence. We are always surrounded by it, immersed in it, sustained by it. God is always present to us—it remains only for us to be present to God.

The only moment we can ever live is the present moment. The only time we have to be happy, to learn, to grow, is this present moment, this present moment, this present moment, this present moment....

CONSIDER:

♦ What does "living in the present moment" mean to me?

♦ When am I totally absorbed (truly present) in what I am doing? Is this a common or a rare experience for me? Why?

♦ How does our life-style help "living in the present moment"? How does it hinder?

A Celebration of Appreciation

There once was a queen who dearly loved the people of her realm. She created for them a lovely garden filled with animals and birds and fishes and growing things of all kinds. Everywhere were things to intrigue and amaze and delight. When the garden was completed, the queen sent forth her servants to invite all the people of her realm to come to enjoy it.

The people came. But some of them refused to look at the beautiful things there, preferring to be absorbed with their own trivial pastimes. Others despoiled the buildings, threw garbage into the waters, polluted the air, vandalized the gardens, and killed the birds and animals and fish for sport.

One of the servants, observing these actions, said to the queen, "Your Majesty, these people do not appreciate what you have done for them. They have no love for your garden; they do not appreciate beauty and wonder; they have abused your generosity. Shall we bind them and cast them from here?"

But the queen answered, "Leave these people to themselves. To refuse to recognize beauty is itself penalty. Ignorance and oblivion are themselves punishment enough."

CONSIDER:

♦ When do I recognize God in creation? Why?

♦ When am I most aware of the earth's beauty and wonder? Most appreciative and grateful?

♦ It has been said that if we cannot appreciate beauty we cannot appreciate liturgy. Do I agree? Why or why not?

A Celebration of the Written Word

What a wonderful gift to be able to read! What a marvelous talent to be able to write! It is only because humanity has developed these two skills that we now have the Scriptures, physically handed down from the past. Those delicate markings, so fragile and perishable, have been preserved, often at great sacrifice to individuals. Some people gave up their lives so that we today would be able to read the word of God.

Through the centuries people have honored and respected Scripture in various ways: Some have studied it; others have laboriously copied it by hand; some have translated it into different languages; others have smuggled banned copies into forbidden areas; still others have set Scripture verses to music.

But we must always make a distinction about what is meant by "the word of God," for Scripture has no meaning if it remains nothing more than markings in a book. The Bible is not a magic talisman in and of itself.

Because we can read and write and speak and sing, the Scriptures form a significant part of our liturgies. Not long ago the liturgical readings concluded with the words "This is the word of the Lord," or "This is the Gospel of the Lord." Some readers would elevate the lectionary for all to see.

Now these declarations have been changed to simply "the word of the Lord" or "the Gospel of the Lord."

The change in wording distinguishes between Scripture contained in a book, and Scripture used in a liturgical setting. Within the liturgy, "the word of the Lord" has a much broader, richer, meaning.

Liturgically speaking, the word of the Lord is always alive and active. Lector, cantor, presider lift it from the ink and paper of the book, give breath and voice to the word, and send it out to us in the assembly.

But simply giving voice to the Scriptures does not make it the word of God in this broader sense—unless it is also received. We, as congregation, are necessary to the proclamation of the word! If the lector practiced reading in an empty church, it would not be the word of the Lord in this sense. Why? Because we, the assembly, would not be there to receive it. But when we are fully present and open, we the assembly *become* the word of God, alive and active. And the Holy Spirit moves through us and in us, touching hearts and minds; the word is alive and fills the room.

We are all proclaimers of the word of God—not just

the lectors, cantors, presiders, preachers. When the eucharistic minister presents to us the broken bread, that minister does not say "*This is* the Body of Christ," for that is too exclusive. Yes, that bread is the Body of Christ, but so too are we.

No longer do the lectors and presiders hold up the lectionary and say "*This is* the word of the Lord," because that is also too exclusive. Yes, that book is the Lord's word, but so too are we.

CONSIDER:

♦ What does "the word of God" mean to me?

♦ How do I react to being considered "the word of God" to those around me?

♦ What we do together at worship we symbolize for each other during the rest of the week. What do the community members symbolize for me? What might I symbolize for them?

A Celebration of the Body of Christ

Way back in the liturgical year—at the later Mass on Christmas Day, when we read John's Gospel and proclaimed Christ, it was not the newborn God-Incarnate that we proclaimed but rather the adult Christ. The Gospel for that Mass drew our attention not to the marvelous happenings in Bethlehem but rather to the marvel of the Incarnation itself: "In the beginning was the Word, and the Word was with God, and the Word was God" (John 1:1).

And what were the primary liturgical symbols of that day? The most important symbols of the Incarnation were not the creche and the familiar figures of the Nativity, but rather the proclamation of the word, the breaking of the bread and the assembly of believers. The Body of Christ which is recognized on the feast of the Nativity is the assembly of believers.

So too now, as we celebrate the risen Christ, we look around us for the most important symbols of the Resurrection. The primary liturgical symbols of this season are not the Easter lily and the Paschal candle and the white vestments—but once again, the proclamation of the word, the breaking of the bread and the assembly of believers. The Body of Christ, the symbol of the risen Christ, is the assembly of believers.

It has been said that Christ died as an individual and rose as a people. This eternal paradox of divinity and humanity, of birth and death, is symbolized by the Body of Christ—the assembly of believers. We, through the Holy Spirit, are the Body of Christ. We are the symbol of the risen Christ.

CONSIDER:

♦ What does the term "Body of Christ" mean to me?

♦ How do the Incarnation and the Resurrection influence my attitude toward my physical body?

♦ How do I feel about being told that I am the Body of Christ?

♦ Looking around the church at the people gathered there, I can think to myself "You people are the Body of Christ." How do I feel about that?

A Celebration of Freedom

Engaging in slave-keeping is not Christian. Slavery is demeaning to the enslaved and corrupting to the enslaver. Slavery is both immoral and illegal. Slavery is also very common.

While formal slavery has been abolished legally, we still manage to enslave one another: children, spouses, parents, family members, friends, coworkers. We hold each other in bondage:

by our expectations of others which, instead of nurturing and encouraging growth, restrict and smother and bind;
by our fears of "the different";
by our imposition of our will over others;
by our desire to conform;
by our fears of creativity;
by our concerns about "what others think";
by our preconceived ideas of what should be;

by our imposition of the burden of our "worry."

If we truly believe in the Holy Spirit, we are forced to admit that the same Spirit is directing not just us but others too. And that unpredictable Holy Spirit may be guiding others, including those close to us, along pathways that we may not choose for them. It is not for us to choose the direction of the Holy Spirit's guidance! It is for us to free others, enabling them to be faithful to the Spirit's call.

CONSIDER:

♦ When have I felt in bondage to another? How was the bondage imposed? How did it affect my actions? My attitudes? My emotions?

♦ How do we hold others in bondage by our concerns about what others may think? By our fears of creativity? By our worry?

♦ When might I have tried to hold another in bondage? How? Why? What was the effect on the other person? What was the result for me?

Favorite

Listen, Beloved!
You are my favorite!
Of all my children, I love you best.

Do you not understand how this can be?
Believe!
I am the realm of the gloriously impossible,
and you are my favorite!

In all of time, you are special to me!
I formed you according to my plan.
I, who have no ordinary children,
have left my mark on you,
the hallmark of the divine.
My image in you can never be lost or erased.

I love you.
I love you as though you were the only person I ever
created!
Do you not understand how this can be?
Believe!
I am the realm of the gloriously impossible,
and you are my favorite!

A Celebration of Ecumenism

With the fervor of Vatican II renewal, we Catholics celebrate our own tradition, rich in spirituality, sacramentality and liturgy. In the same life-giving spirit, we have come to recognize the gifts which other religions bring to humanity's understanding and worship of the divine. Other believers, in vast numbers or in few, offer their own unique gifts.

The Jews offer their unique heritage as God's chosen people. The Muslims present faithfulness to daily prayer and to fasting. The members of the Orthodox Churches present reverent divine liturgies and faith-filled participation in the Trinitarian mystery.

The Lutherans present devotion to the grace of the Triune God made known through word and sacrament. The Anglicans offer a unique combination of Catholic heritage and Protestant conscience. The members of the Presbyterian and Reform churches offer faithfulness to God's covenant and reverence for moral law.

The Methodists bring their awakening of Christian social conscience and emphasis upon witnessing. The Baptist, Evangelical and Pentecostal Churches offer missionary zeal and the recognition of the mature soul's relation to God. Other Christians offer proclamation of the gospel of salvation through repentance and the inspiration of conscientious lives.

The people of the United Church of Christ present their emphasis on the free movement of the Holy Spirit and on preaching. The Disciples of Christ bring their emphasis on individual freedom and on ecumenism. The Moravians bring their wonderful hymn-singing. The Amish present reminders of the value of simplicity.

The Universalists present their affirmation in the ultimate salvation of all. The Quakers offer traditions of religious equality and of faith in the Holy Spirit. The Salvation Army presents its dedication to bringing the gospel to those untouched by the other Churches.

Jehovah's Witnesses offer a steadfast zeal for evangelization. The Mormons offer generosity to the Church and concern for the welfare of the community. The Christian Scientists offer resolute faith in the Divine Healer.

The Buddhists bring awareness, enlightenment, meditation. The Hindus present the delightful tradition of seeing the exceedingly numerous faces of God. The Taoists offer "The Way" and the study of the inner nature. The Baha'is offer their dedication to the collective sanctity of the entire human race. The Shintoists bring a reverence for ancestors and family. The Confucians offer emphasis upon right order, ethics and the harmonization of opposites.

The many primordial religions offer respect for nature and recognition of God in creation. The members of the goddess faiths witness to the feminine, inclusive, life-bringing nature of God. The practitioners of spiritual principles emphasize the divine omnipresence and the consciousness of God-within. The new religions offer their challenges to rethink, restructure, revise.

Humanists offer their deep respect for reason. Finally, agnostics and atheists, by their very presence, testify to the value of courage and honesty in the God-quest.

Ecumenism values the gifts of all God's family that bring insight to our understanding of ourselves and God. Without diminishing our own religious commitment, we honor these gifts.

CONSIDER:

♦ What specific, personal gifts of faith do I bring to those around me?

♦ What specific, personal gifts of faith have I received from people of other faiths?

♦ What gifts of faith do I feel my Church brings to my larger community? To the world?

♦ What gifts do I especially appreciate in other faiths?

A Celebration of Who I Am

W ho am I?
I am what I do.
My job, profession, the tasks I perform—all help define me. I am what I do each day, each week.
Who am I?
I am also what I desire to do. I am what I desire to do—even if now I have no opportunity to do these things.

Who am I?
I am also what I dream.
My dreams—are they not the whisperings of the Holy
Spirit?
Who am I?
I am a person in relationship.
I am a child, grandchild, great-grandchild in a family.
I may be brother, sister, aunt, uncle, cousin.
I may be husband, wife, parent, grandparent.
Who am I?
I am more than a doer;
I am more than a person in a family.
I am a believer, a Christian, a Catholic. I have been
made in God's image.
And God looked at what had been created and saw that
it was good!
Who am I?
I am graced with God's presence.
The very breath that sustains me is the breath of the
Holy Spirit.
Christ dwells within me.
It is here, within, that I find my worth.
It is here I find the reason for my being.
Who am I?
I am a being created out of love.
I have been created to love and to be loved.
God loves me in my grief and in my joy.
Who am I?
And now, this moment, I do nothing but allow God to
love me.
I open myself up and allow God's love to fill me.
I allow myself to feel God's love—
God's unconditional love.

CONSIDER:

♦ The above.

♦ Who am I?

♦ Who do I want to be? Why? What prevents me from making the changes?

A Celebration of the Gospel

Theirs is a most unusual family—unique in both size and makeup—for Vicky and David are the parents of seventeen children, most of whom are adopted. All of these chosen children had been considered unadoptable, either because of mixed racial heritage or because of handicaps. One boy was born with no arms, one child has no kidneys and is completely dependent on dialysis, another is legally blind, another retarded. Their family picture could be used for a united charities appeal!

A friend once asked Vicky to write her interpretation of the gospel. Vicky smiled and answered, "Look at my life! My life is my interpretation of the gospel."

We can all say, "My life is my interpretation of the gospel," for our lives do reflect our beliefs. That's an intimidating thought! It seems appropriate to make that statement about people like Vicky and Dave, but for the rest of us?

Yet, in another way, it is also affirming. What we are and what we do are important. With our lives we are writing a sentence or two in the continuing saga of salvation history. We are interpreters of the gospel; we are theologians; we are moral philosophers. By our lives we are all proclaiming the word of God. Not just ordained priests and professed religious, not just lectors and cantors and preachers, but all of us who are Christians share in the priesthood of Christ and proclaim the word of God by our lives.

We are the word of God in the world. And when that challenge seems overwhelming, where can we go for needed guidance and strength? We can turn to the word of the God in Scripture and to the word of the God embodied in community. We are the word of God for each other.

CONSIDER:

♦ How do I feel about the statement that my life reflects my interpretation of the gospel?

♦ How would someone else "read" the gospel of my life?

♦ Whom do I know personally whose life reflects the gospel message for me? Why?

A Celebration of Mystery

God is the divine, eternal Mystery. God cannot be wholly contained in our concepts, described in our words, bracketed in our thoughts, compressed within our imaginations. God is simplicity and paradox; God is the Alpha and the Omega; God is ying and yang; God is within time and outside of time.

God is the "I Am Who Am!" How we struggle with language to convey that existence which is God! We experiment with words trying to discover some way to say that God *is*; we search for a yet undiscovered superlative of the verb *to be*.

He/She/It/They: God! We search for the correct pronoun to use in reference to our Triune God, discovering that there is no single pronoun sufficient for such Mystery.

God is "I Will Be Who I Will Be." We recognize, we celebrate, but we do not understand the mystery of God. God is the sacred, transcendent yet immanent; God is the One apart, yet embodied in the sacredness of all people.

We are addicted to imaging a human-like God—but the commandment against idolatry forbids us to do so. It is this mystery of God, this mystery of the Trinity, which rescues us from picturing God in an all-too-human form. We are not to neglect the *mystery* of God.

Knowing that a complete understanding of God is beyond us, still we struggle to experience and feel the presence of God. We learn that we cannot grasp, we can only approach. We use metaphors, knowing that they are always less than the reality. We learn to image God beyond our imaging. We learn to imagine and to reimagine.

God is God!

CONSIDER:

♦ What are some of the ways in which we today violate the commandment forbidding idolatry?

♦ How do I respond to people who profess to know and understand the workings of God?

♦ How do I keep alive for myself the mystery of God?

A Celebration of Cloisters

The monastic tradition is a well-established part of Catholicism. For centuries men and women have entered the religious orders to devote their lives to prayer in cloister.

We have all encountered wonderful, inspirational writings and talks on prayer. We know there are passages in Scripture about prayer and its necessity to our lives. Yet, can any of these be as powerful an influence upon us as the example of these praying people? Every day of our life, we know that these women and men of the monastic tradition are praying for us around the clock.

Early in the morning, while we are still struggling to respond to the miracle of a new day, we are remembered in prayer. Through the morning hours, whether playing as a child, studying as a student, working as a laborer, we are remembered in prayer. Gobbling a hurried lunch as a much-distracted parent, an experiment-watching scientist, an intensely focused business meeting participant, we are remembered in prayer.

In early afternoon, as a reluctantly resting child or a neglected person with a disability or a sick adolescent or a bored assembly worker or a weary oldster, we are remembered in prayer. As the afternoon progresses and we enter the rush-hour congestion, whether homeward bound or to the late-shift job, we are remembered in prayer. During the dinner-hour, as we cook or wait tables or direct traffic or nurse the infirm, we are remembered in prayer.

In the hours of evening, as we relax or work or study or make love or care for others, we are remembered in prayer. During the midnight hours, whether sleeping, or anxiously awaiting the teen with the car, or keeping sickroom vigil or participating in our work world, we are remembered in prayer.

However we spend our God-given time—as artist or engineer, pilot or truck driver or physician, caregiver or care-recipient, social activist or full-time parent, migrant worker or teacher or clerk or animal caretaker or musician, secretary or laborer or nonworker, manager or scientist or church worker or sailor, fixer or cleaner or builder, entertainer or writer or farmer, bureaucrat or retiree—we are remembered in prayer.

No matter if we are just entering life or about to leave it, no matter if we are married or single, no matter if we are believers or nonbelievers or doubters, no matter if we are lonely or smothered in relationships, no matter if we are overwhelmed with sorrow or joy or anxiety, we know that somewhere someone is praying for us.

As we come to realize the significance of the pray-ers and the power of their prayers, we also realize our own obligation to pray. And so we are privileged to join with them in praying for all those in need, in praying for the world, in praying to praise God.

CONSIDER:

♦ Do I feel connected in prayer with those within the cloisters? Why or why not?

♦ What responsibilities do I feel for praying for others?

♦ Is the praise of God part of my prayer life? Why or why not?

A Celebration of Empowerment

The ultimate and supreme act of empowerment is bringing forth life from death. Thus did the Spirit empower Christ in the Resurrection; thus will the Spirit empower us in the final resurrection.

But while awaiting this future unsurpassable act of empowerment, we cannot neglect our own opportunities to empower others and to be empowered ourselves. This task of compassionately empowering others is ours by our sharing in the priesthood of Christ—it is ours by Baptism.

God does not give us gifts to be hidden or abused; God does not bestow upon us talents to be drowned in false humility. Within each of us are dormant seeds of creativity and potential and talents and virtues waiting only for the right conditions to sprout and grow. When we empower one another we bring these gifts to fruition.

Parents have years of ample opportunities to empower their children. Spouses can empower each other within that most intimate and loving relationship. Friends, in the true spirit of friendship, can empower one another.

The real power of community lies in each and every member's utilizing the many opportunities to nurture, sustain, encourage one another. This empowerment builds up the Body of Christ and always involves the Holy Spirit and those delightfully surprising and challenging and creative gifts/fruits/graces of the Spirit.

The Body of Christ needs the fulfillment of the

potential of each of us.

CONSIDER:

- How do I experience empowerment? In what areas of my life?

- Who has empowered me? How? What was the result?

- Whom do I empower? How?

- Whom else could I help empower? How?

FIFTH SUNDAY OF EASTER

Roots

Listen, Beloved!
Unless your life is rooted in me,
you live superficially.

The plants which I created
instinctively reach upward;
they reach for light and air—
needed for survival.

The plants which I created
also reach downward;
they reach for moisture—
needed for survival.

So you too, Beloved,
instinctively reach for me,
your Creator,
for without me
you cannot live fully.

Believe in me.
Each day, believe in me.
Do not wait for crises,
do not wait for challenges
that seem beyond your strength.
Believe in me.

Follow my light,

that you may see the way.
Nourish yourself on the food I have given you:
my body as bread and wine,
my word,
my community,
my Spirit within you.

Sink your roots deep into me.
I am the ground of creation,
the source of all life,
the wellspring of grace.

Unless your life is rooted in me,
Beloved,
you live superficially.
Live in me!

A Celebration of Mountain Climbers

We are surrounded everywhere by mountain climbers—the many people for whom each day means confronting a Matterhorn or an Everest.

There are the "other-abled," challenged by living in a world constructed for the seeing, hearing, fully-limbed, physically capable. There are the developmentally delayed, whose understanding much of our complicated and sophisticated culture exceeds.

There are the recovering addicts, clinging to normalcy one day, one hour, one minute at a time. There are the victims of phobias and demons and disease and age and prejudice and loneliness and nightmare realities who survive in spite of all.

These people climb a mountain each day. Usually their climb is unrecognized and unapplauded, yet they, even more than the obviously adventuresome, testify to the presence of the Holy Spirit in our midst.

Actually climbing the Matterhorn or Kilimanjaro or Denali or Everest requires of the climbers courage and faith and endurance. But for the mountain climbers mentioned above, all these virtues are necessary just to survive the demands of everyday life. Many of these people accomplish the feat not through their own strength but through their weakness; not through their own courage, but their admitted fear; not through their own endurance, but their frailty.

For the rest of us, what usually hinders the expression of the goodness and compassion of God in our lives is the misplaced faith we affirm in our own strength and ability. It is our pride-filled dependence upon our own efforts that blocks the working of the Holy Spirit. Only when we are confronted with climbing a mountain do we call upon the God within and everywhere and see God in all.

These mountain climbers have no choice but to accept the realities of their lives, willingly plunge into the pain and actually embrace the mountain. Only then does the mountain become transformed and, like the mountaintop Transfiguration, reveal the presence of God.

- Who are the "mountain climbers" in my life? How do they inspire me? What have I learned from them?

- What do I do to encourage and sustain them?

- What can I do to help other "mountain climbers"?

A Celebration of Our Divine Parentage

Our words and poetry, our visual art, our music, cannot contain or describe God. Like an icon, however, each attempt provides us with one way of visualizing our many-faceted God; each may be correct, but only in a limited and finite way. It is the cumulative addition of image to image, icon to icon, that more accurately describes God, for in our fumbling, finite world, we are attempting to put limitless Being within the confines of words and definitions.

The power and universality of the Almighty cannot be confined to one humanly defined concept, no matter how carefully it is described, no matter how perfectly idealized.

God is to us as a *father*: protecting and providing, patient and wise, disciplining and life-sustaining, loving and most worthy of respect. God holds us in the palm of his hand.

God is to us as a *mother*: nurturing and maternal and gentle, strong and immanent and sacrificing, sheltering us in her womb, nursing us at her breast. God refuses to allow her children to be lost.

God is to us as a *grandfather*: accepting and empowering, interested, bragging, longing and laughing and kind, teaching, understanding, generous. God accepts us, just as we are, unconditionally.

God is to us as a *grandmother*: doting, spoiling, faithful, listening, loving, caressing, affectionate, delighting, never too busy. God loves us with a love that cannot be alienated, a love that knows no measure or season or time.

Through the prophet Jeremiah God has said, "I have loved you with an everlasting love" (31:3b). Because God is and always was, God is our Father/Mother and our Grandfather/Grandmother and....

CONSIDER:

♦ Which are my favorite images of God? Why?

♦ How have my life experiences influenced my preference for those God images?

♦ How do my favorite images limit God? How can I expand my concept of God?

A Celebration of the Sabbath

The divine example is given to us early in Scripture. In the very first book of the Hebrew Scriptures, Genesis 2:2 states that God rested. After the work of creation, God rested.

The important point is not which day, or the detailed specifics of what is forbidden and what is allowed. What is important is our observance of a Sabbath—a day of rest, a day of praising God in community.

The command to have a day of rest is not a restriction of our freedom but a recognition of our need as human beings; it is a command given for our own good. Thomas Merton has referred to our busyness as the violence we do to ourselves. Our observance of a Sabbath limits or prevents this violence.

We need to rest. We need to look over what we have done and note its goodness, and then rest. We need to work for beauty and justice, contemplate what we have done, and then rest. We need to labor in a loving fashion to spread the Good News, verify that our activities are in harmony with God's creation, and then join in God's resting. That's when we discover that rest has a dignity and value all its own. That is Sabbath.

"The Holy One, blessed be He, said to Moses: 'Moses! I have a precious gift in my treasure house. Its name is Shabbat and I want to give it to the Israelites, go and inform them' (Babylonian Talmud, Shabbat 10b). For those who have accepted that gift, Shabbat continues to be a day of delight and spiritual renewal."[1]

We need a day to celebrate the liturgy in community and thus honor all that the liturgy celebrates: creation and the Creator, the Incarnation, the Paschal Mystery, the Holy Spirit, our blessings, the mystery of us.

CONSIDER:

♦ When do I rest? Can I rest without feeling guilty?

♦ Is my time away from work frenetic time? Refreshing time? Relaxing time?

♦ Is all my time full of activity?

♦ Is there a state of being for me that I regularly visit—somewhere between activity and sleep? Have I discovered that place?

♦ Is there such a place for each member of my family? Do all family members have an opportunity to visit their place frequently and when they wish?

---

[1] Hillel Foundation of Cambridge, Inc. *The Harvard Hillel Sabbath Songbook.* (Boston: David R. Godine, Publisher, Inc., 1992), p. xi.

A Celebration of the Council

C elebrate the Second Vatican Council!
Celebrate the Spirit-filled, Spirit-led
Council! Celebrate the openness, freshness,
vibrancy of the Council!

Celebrate the *aggiornamento*—the updating—
accomplished by the Council. Celebrate the courage
of the Council!

Celebrate the traditions honored by the Council!

Celebrate the diversity of the worldwide Church of
the Council! Celebrate the oneness of the Mystical
Body of Christ—the Church of the Council!

Celebrate the new Pentecost of the Council!

Celebrate the ecumenism of the Council!
Celebrate the religious freedom recognized by the
Council!

Celebrate the growth—the risky, fearful,
unpredicted, courageous, amazing growth—since the
Council! Celebrate the path undertaken in faith by the
Council! Celebrate in faith the path that lies ahead for
us—the Church of the Council!

CONSIDER:

♦ From my own experience or from what I have
learned, how would I characterize the pre-Vatican II
Church?

♦ What documents of the Vatican II Council have I
read? How did I respond?

- What more do I need to learn about the Council and all that has followed?

- What do I most appreciate about the changes begun by Vatican II? What do I appreciate least?

- How do I envision the Church of the future?

A Celebration of Imagination

What if I were God? Would I have created a universe? Would I have fashioned stars and planets and galaxies—all set within this complexity of physical laws?

If I were God, would I have created such a diversity of creatures? Creatures that fly and swim and crawl; creatures that roar and squawk and sing and chirp and squeak and chatter; creatures so awesome and comical; so magnificent; so tiny? How much control would I want to have over my creation and creatures?

If I were God, would I have had the courage to create creatures like humans? Would I have blessed them with such beautiful bodies, with their awesome senses and marvelous sexuality? Would I have been so profligate as to give them free will? Would I have created humanity in my own image? Would I be embarrassed or angry or hurt by the actions of people?

How would I communicate with all my creatures? How would I communicate with people? How could I show love to people?

If I were God, would I have become a human being for their sake? Would I have come to earth to teach them how to live? Would I have been willing to suffer and die for them?

If I really were God, would I remain in Spirit with my people throughout all of time? Would I continue to sustain, nourish, love my people?

If I were God, how would I expect them to treat each other? What would I personally expect from my people? And, if I really were God, how would I feel about the happenings in the world today?

CONSIDER:

♦ What, for me, would be the hardest part of being God? Why?

♦ What would I most enjoy doing, if I were God? Why?

♦ What would I do differently? Why?

A Celebration of Fervor

Fervor is the fire of Pentecost transforming Christ's fearful followers into bold proclaimers of the word. Fervor is the love of God overflowing into love of neighbor. Fervor is the faith welling up inside us until it spills over into action.

Fervor is not represented by the cautious, comfortable Christian. Its representatives are the brave Stephen, the first martyr; the New Testament widow giving her mite to the temple; Damien working with the lepers; Thomas More defying Henry VIII; Joan of Arc leading an army; Dorothy Day working in the slums or Archbishop Oscar Romero boldly preaching the gospel. Fervor is going beyond the reasonable, the practical, the prudent. Fervor is the lone individual standing before the armed military tank—whether that tank be a literal weapon or a figurative one of bureaucracy or hostility or social convention.

Fervor is almsgiving—not from surplus but from substance. It is involvement even when the cost is pain. It is the compassion that reopens the giver's scars. It is forgiveness—not only of friends, but of enemies as well. It is the total abandonment to God's will; it is the presence of the Holy Spirit in our lives.

While most of us will not be challenged to shed our blood as martyrs or to endure the hardships of adventurous Paul or to be as self-sacrificing as Maximilian Kolbe, we do need the inspiration of their examples to meet our own hardships and challenges. We need the same kind of courageous fervor to be truly committed Christians: risking social embarrassment or rejection, overcoming shyness, picking ourselves up after failure, contributing generously of our time and money and effort, maintaining our standards in the face of pressure, believing that no situation is hopeless.

Fervor is making a Spirit-inspired commitment to the gospel.

CONSIDER:

♦ How do I define fervor? How does it differ from
emotionalism?

♦ Whom do I know who exemplifies fervor? How do I
respond to that person?

♦ When have I been overcome with fervor? How did it
feel? What was the result?

God-Like

Listen, Beloved!

You are not God.
I—and only I—am God.

Yet, you are like me,
for I have made you in my image.

When you love,
you are like me.

When you forgive,
you are like me.

When you lose yourself in unselfishness,
you are like me.

When you are creative,
you are like me.

When you are life-giving,
you are like me.

When you are nurturing,
you are like me.

When you bless,
you are like me.

So, bless one another!
Use the talents I have given you

to bless one another.
Give to all
what I have given to each of you.

You are very like me,
Beloved.

A Celebration of Creativity

Nothing in all of known history is more creative than creation. Nothing known since then has surpassed that feat!

God was and is both the first artist and the ultimate artist. God continues to sing and dance and paint throughout the universe, to act in stories, to write the tale of salvation history.

Not only did God create the universe and everything in it, but God continues to create other creatures—human beings—imbued with that marvelous creativity too. We have imagination and inventiveness and vision and the ability to see the beyond. It is our creative potential that is the image of God within us.

The geniuses among us cannot survive without giving expression to their creativity—this is as necessary to them as food or air. Everyone, however, has some degree of creativity. Our thoughts and feelings and actions all have elements of creativity, for that is our heritage.

Creativity is not mainly an expression of our

knowledge—though that may be utilized in our creativity. Nor is creativity primarily an expression of our skills and talents—though these, too, may be utilized in our creative activities. The most holy art of creativity comes from who we *are*, for when we are in the state of creating, undiminished by distraction, we are acting from our *being*. It is our being that produces the creative; it is from who we are, through the Holy Spirit, that creativity flows. That is why it is most like God, the One who is and ever shall be.

When we are in the Spirit-led state of creating, we are lost to self-consciousness and pride; we simply are. That's why the doing of creative action is its own reward.

That's also why creating is always risky. Thus some people fear or even forbid creativity, for it is unpredictable and cannot be preprogrammed. The Holy Spirit, that Dove of creativity, has yet to be domesticated!

All that we create reflects back to our Creator and to the Spirit within us. Johann Sebastian Bach, a musical creative genius, recognized this by endorsing his compositions: "All for the honor and glory of God."

CONSIDER:

♦ How do I define or describe creativity? What is my attitude toward the creativity of others? How do I support the creativity of those around me?

♦ How do I feel about my own creativity? How do I express my creativity?

A Celebration of the Paschal Mystery

The cycle of life, as it is usually described, is from life to death; we are born, we live, we die. We are ever in the presence of death, faced with embracing our mortality.

But the Paschal Mystery tells us that the complete cycle of life goes from life to life; we are born, we live, we die to be born into eternal life.

> Christ has died,
> Christ is risen,
> Christ will come again!

Within our own lives we experience, in the continuous flow of life-to-death-to-life, a foretaste of the Paschal Mystery. We begin one life phase, complete it, go on to another; we enter into relationships that grow, ebb, end, leaving time and space for others. We experience varied conversions and transitions throughout our lifetime. Each birth is painful, anxious, joyous; each death is traumatic and agonizing and freeing.

> Lord, by your cross and resurrection
> you have set us free.
> You are the Savior of the world!

We come to the major interchanges of our life journey and experience a dying to the old self and a rising of the new through the Holy Spirit. We experience change, movement, growth, increasing maturity.

When we eat this bread and drink this cup,
we proclaim your death, Lord Jesus,
until you come in glory!

If there is one idea, one theme, one leitmotif which is
the meditation of Christian life, it is the Paschal
Mystery: the living and dying and rising of Christ, the
daily little deaths of woundedness and limitation and
failure, our own final dying and rising.

Now, in this Eastertide, we celebrate the rebirth of
life and love, freedom and faith in Christ. Resurrection
is victory in death, for death is the portal through
which we must pass to resurrection. The final chapter
of the Paschal Mystery will see the coming of the
cosmic Christ at the end of time.

Dying you destroyed our death,
rising you restored our life.
Lord Jesus, come in glory!

CONSIDER:

♦ When have I experienced a dying and rising in my
life? What were the various emotions that I
experienced? How long was it before I could see the
larger context of the event?

♦ How can I assist someone who is going through a
Good Friday? What can I say or do to sustain this
person?

A Celebration of Wisdom

Somewhere, in that mutual community of love that we call the Trinity, is the Holy Spirit—that nebulous, multifaceted, obscure, necessary person of the Triune God. We are ever searching for ways to describe that ever-present Third Person of the Trinity.

The Holy Spirit is intimately involved in the Incarnation and the Paschal Mystery, taking part in Christ's conception, Baptism, Resurrection and, of course, Pentecost.

Traditionally the Holy Spirit is the bringer of the special fruits of love, joy, peace, patient endurance, kindness, generosity, faith, mildness and chastity (see Galatians 5:22-23a). In addition, the Spirit is the bestower of the gifts of wisdom, understanding, counsel, fortitude, knowledge, piety, fear of the Lord (see Isaiah 11:2).

In Hebrew, the Spirit is feminine, as is Wisdom in both Hebrew and Greek. Thus one metaphor for the Spirit is Lady Wisdom or Sophia—which is Greek for "wisdom." Wisdom/Sophia is present before creation; Yahweh looked for Sophia before beginning the work of creation.

The mystics know Sophia; they exuberantly dance with Sophia, who is full of surprises, playful, a lover of delight. This metaphor for the divine, Lady Wisdom, dances through the universe among the stars, creating and inspiring wherever she goes.

The whimsical God of joy, the capricious divine lover, the freedom-seeking promptings of the oppressed, the poets' wind of inspiration, the fire-breathing animating force of equality-seeking humanity—all these are Sophia, the Holy Spirit.

CONSIDER:

♦ How do I envision the activity of the Holy Spirit?

♦ Which gifts or fruits do I most value? Why? Which gifts or fruits do I least value? Why?

♦ In what ways does Sophia reflect for me the feminine face of God?

♦ When have I been most aware of the activity of Sophia?

ASCENSION

A Celebration of Sky-Watching

Why do you stand here looking up at the skies?
(Acts 1:11)

The angels questioned the disciples' lack of activity following the Ascension. "Why do you stand looking up toward heaven?" they asked, for it was time for Jesus' followers to be bringing forth the reign of God.

There are times when it is right and proper to sky-watch; there are occasions when looking up at the heavens is the awesomely appropriate activity.

And so we sky-watch:

to note the progress of a rapidly gathering storm;
to admire the beauty and order of the stars on
  a clear night;
to re-establish our perspectives and priorities;
to admire the ever-fascinating aurora borealis;
to search for an overdue plane;
to cloud-watch—with imagination;
to find peace;
to realize our own insignificance;
to recall our own importance—that our God
  became incarnate;
to establish directions when we are lost;
to follow the course of a kite;

to note bird migration;
to track satellites and space vehicles;
to remind ourselves of the vastness of the
    universe;
to realize how much God loves us.

"Why do you stand looking up toward heaven?"
    "Angels," we answer, "we have many exemplary
reasons for our sky-watching."
    Yet no matter the justification for our heavenward
looking, we, no less than the apostles, must move from
watching to tending, from observing to participating,
from meditation to ministering. It is time for us, too, to
be bringing forth the reign of God.

CONSIDER:

♦ When do I stand "looking up toward heaven"? Why?

♦ When do I "sky-watch" figuratively?

♦ What effect does my sky-watching have?

♦ What actions are prompted by my sky-watching?

♦ How am I helping to bring forth the reign of God?

A Celebration of the Reverence for Life

I n the Hindu faith the sacredness of all life is a very important belief. There is a reason for each and every life God placed on the earth.

Many Hindus, finding the mere thought of killing and eating another creature quite repugnant, are vegetarians. How arrogant to them is the assumption that other animals were put on this earth for our consumption! But this recognition of the sacredness of life is not restricted to the larger forms of life. Very devout Hindus, when walking in the open air, wear a gauze strip in front of their mouths lest in the necessary act of breathing they accidentally inhale a gnat or fly and so deprive even such an insignificant— to us—creature of its chance to live its full God-given life.

Such respect for life has not been a major thrust of our Euro-Christian tradition, for our history depicts a rather ruthless attitude toward much of creation. We set out to "subdue" the earth and to show every living thing who's boss!

We have forgotten, ignored or perhaps never realized one very important fact of life: *We* are the ones who are most in need of the rest of creation! If the human race disappeared from the face of the earth, the plant life, the animal life, the creatures that swim and fly—all would breathe a collective cosmic sigh of relief and then continue quite well without us.

Now, confronted with possible ecological

cataclysm, we are being challenged to reconsider our position. We are beginning to realize that all life is to be in balance. God, who is ever transcendent, is also immanent throughout our universe. Perhaps our model is not to be one of hierarchical domination, but cooperative harmony and interdependence.

CONSIDER:

♦ How does the Hindu regard for life compare to our American/Christian attitudes?

♦ How "Christian" is our popular attitude toward all of God's creation?

♦ How "Christian" is our acceptance of violence in our society and in the media?

♦ Where does materialism fit into the ecological picture?

♦ What ecological responsibilities do I have as a Christian? In my job/profession? As a member of the human race?

A Celebration of Mary

She was there!

She was there—
need it be said—
at Annunciation-time,
with that daring leap of faith "Yes!"
Mary, so young a woman,
becoming the first to declare herself
a Spirit-sanctioned Christian!

Mary was there at the Nativity,
the new mother elevating the consecrated human-
   divine being
and proclaiming
"The Body of Christ"!

She was there at Cana,
where, as a Jewish mother confident of her son's
   obedience,
she serenely requests a miracle.

Mary was there at the preaching and teaching and
   healing;
Mary was there in the hustling, crowded times;
Mary was there in the solitary moments.

She was there at the crucifixion,
clothed in impregnable courage;
she was there at the burial—
keen, Mary, keen!

Mary,
survivor in faith,

outlasted that destitution
to celebrate the Resurrection—
Alleluia!

And she was there at Pentecost—
never having forgotten her private visitation
from that ever-indwelling Presence.

Did Mary too "speak in tongues"?
Did she, the original Christian,
evangelize for her Son, her God?
What did Mary,
whose first Pentecost heralded the birth of Christ,
foresee in this Pentecost?

Mary was there
when the young Christians gathered at table,
offering together the bread and the wine,
becoming one in the body she had birthed.

Mary was there,
that all ages—
ours no less than others—
should call her blessed.

CONSIDER:

♦ What is my usual image of Mary? Where did I
  acquire this image?

♦ How do I envision Mary after the Resurrection?
  How do I envision her in the company of the new
  Christians? How do I envision Mary evangelizing?

◆ Where is Mary in my relationship with God? Why?

A Celebration of the Elderly

We who are the Church, we who are community, need the diversity of the generations.

We live in the present—and the Spirit is here. And of course we celebrate the young in age and the young in faith who give us hope and renew us. But we also celebrate the elderly of our community who offer to us their gifts.

We honor the older members of our community for their experience, for their strong spiritual essence, for their longer-range perspective, for their faithfulness. We honor their wisdom, a wisdom that recognizes grace, recognizes the necessity of faith in God, in family and friends, in oneself.

The elderly are proof to us of the Paschal Mystery; by their life-experiences they testify that the various Good Fridays of human existence do lead, eventually, to resurrections.

As the older members of the community they are bridges to the past. Through the power of memory, they can transform legacies from previous times into understandable living elements of the present. They are our roots, forming who and what we are today.

The elderly teach effectively by their courage in old age and the faith with which they approach death.

As they embrace their own mortality they are life-mentors for us all; we recognize their role as models.

Of course not all elderly people are paragons of virtue, yet they all have value for us. The bitter ones remind us to prioritize our time and efforts; the apathetic ones stimulate us to live life passionately; the angry ones prompt us to choose carefully our responses to life; the unfulfilled ones remind us to live life with enthusiasm; the unhappy ones provoke us to look for the good in everyone and every situation.

We honor our elderly by recognizing their abilities and their wisdom and by providing opportunities for them to give their gifts to the entire community—and especially to the young, so that there may be mutual benefits of cross-generational involvement.

We express our gratitude to the elderly in the community for their many legacies to us and to the world.

CONSIDER:

♦ What are the gifts which only the elderly can give?

♦ How does our society show respect to the elderly? How does our society discount the value of the elderly?

♦ How have I been especially influenced by an elderly person? How have I "repaid" that person?

♦ What can I do to show respect and gratitude to the older members of my community?

This Day

Listen, Beloved!

Today, this day,
is an original,
a one-of-a-kind day.

Today, this day,
begin anew.

Today, this day,
forget the errors of the past—
they are gone.

Today, this day,
forgive yourself—
for I have forgiven you.

Today, this day,
do not worry about lack—
I am your all-sufficiency.

Today, this day,
remember that no good effort,
insignificant though it may seem,
is ever in vain,
for I take note of it.

Today, this day,
know that it is you

who are of value to me.

Today,
embrace with love,
accept with joy,
this day.

A Celebration of Generosity

The story, both true and too common, is of a
widow miserly in her ways. Her grown
grandchildren would exchange tales of visits to
Grandma's and of her miserliness: the multilayered
furniture coverings, the allotted one sheet of toilet
paper and the single serving of food, the bags of bags
and boxes of boxes.

But some of the grandkids' stories lacked any
humorous element, such as the destitute college
student's unsuccessful efforts in seeking financial
help: "But Grandma, I'm not asking you to *give* me the
money—it would be a *loan!*"

When the woman died, a significant hoard of
money was left to the grandchildren, who were now
grown and leading busy, productive lives as a teacher,
a dentist, a lawyer and a chemist. The response was
unanimous: Each of them refused every penny!

If the grandmother thought that her monetary
legacy would insure her being remembered fondly by
her grandchildren, she was mistaken. Grandma had
fine-drawn her legacy through the years, and her

miserliness had etched itself too deeply upon the young to be altered with one dramatic gesture.

As water, given time, marks even stone, so daily life and our living of it etches the memories of those around us. Generosity—or its lack—influences all our words and actions within both family and community; like a strong seasoning put into a stew, it flavors every element of life.

Generosity is not frivolousness or irresponsibility. Neither is the lack of generosity simply miserliness. The presence or absence of generosity is most effectively communicated! It is through our generosity with time, goods, talent or money, that we communicate our priorities. It is through generosity that we say "I love you"; "You are very important to me"; or "I believe in you and in your dreams."

CONSIDER:

♦ When have I been the unexpected recipient of someone's generosity?

♦ When have I been the unexpected victim of someone's miserliness?

♦ On a scale of one (miserly) to ten (generous), how might I be rated by my family? My friends and neighbors? My coworkers? My community?

A Celebration of Our Bodies

I t is the Resurrection that authenticates our
celebration of the Incarnation. The two events
combined validate the sacred worth of our
physical being.

We are to celebrate our thrice-blessed bodiliness!
We have been blessed by having come from the womb
of God; we have been blessed by having shared this
earth with the Incarnate One; we have been blessed by
being the dwelling place of the Holy Spirit. How
blessed are we!

And so we celebrate our embodiment: our physical
abilities and our senses, our differences and our
similarities, our limitations and our glorious
potentials. Surely we have been as Psalm 139 says,
fearfully and wonderfully made!

We celebrate our embodiment: our sensuality and
our sexuality, our passions and our desire for
intimacy. Of such is our longing for God: In sexuality
is a revelatory, sacramental spirituality. This is what it
means to be human!

We are so accustomed to the statement that we
have been made in the image of God, the *imago Dei*,
that it becomes trite. Yet this is not just a reference to
our soul or to our spiritual being. How easy to forget
the repeated scriptural injunctions against creating
images of God. Thus, how intense is the affirmation of
human dignity—the complete human being—that *we*
have been created in God's image!

♦ In what ways does our culture recognize the value of our bodiliness? In what ways does our culture show disdain for our physical nature?

♦ What is my own attitude toward my body? How do I treat my body?

♦ How do I communicate to others my attitude toward my body? Toward our physical humanity?

A Celebration of Our Spaceship Earth

We, aboard our spaceship Earth, are hurtling through the universe at an incredible speed, ever turning on an axis as we encircle the sun. Those who have been privileged to view this planet from space have been tremendously affected by the experience.

These space travelers, of various nationalities and backgrounds, left our earthly confines as scientists and engineers and technicians, as explorers and national patriots; they returned having been forged into poets and humanitarians and world patriots.

The Earth was small, light blue, and so touchingly alone, our home that must be defended like a holy relic. (Aleksei Leonov, U.S.S.R.)

A Chinese tale tells of some men sent to harm a young girl who, upon seeing her beauty, become her protectors rather than her violators. That's how I felt seeing the Earth for the first time. "I could not help but love and cherish her." (Taylor Wang, China/U.S.A.)

From space I saw Earth—indescribably beautiful with the scars of national boundaries gone. (Muhammad Ahmad Faris, Syria)

The first day or so we all pointed to our countries. The third or fourth day we were pointing to our continents. By the fifth day we were aware of only one Earth. (Sultan Bin Salman al-Saud, The Kingdom of Saudi Arabia)

For those who have seen the Earth from space,..... The things that we share in our world are far more valuable than those which divide us. (Donald Williams, U.S.A.)

Before I flew I was already aware of how small and vulnerable our planet is; but only when I saw it from space, in all its ineffable beauty and fragility, did I realize that humankind's most urgent task is to cherish and preserve it for future generations. (Sigmund Jähn, German Democratic Republic)

CONSIDER:

♦ When am I most aware of the sacredness of the Earth?

♦ Where do I envision God with respect to creation: In creation? Above creation? Manipulating creation?

Distant from creation? In a different relationship?

♦ What do I think my reaction would be to the astronauts' experiences?

A Celebration of the Liturgy

The word *liturgy* means "the work of the people." Our Sunday Liturgy:

is the gathering of the baptized to worship God;
shapes our theology;
expresses our theology;
celebrates what is;
celebrates what is to be as though it already is;
is the only hour in the entire week in which we
    are not working at salvation—we are
    celebrating it;
expresses our faith in the Triune God;
is the public memory of the People of God;
celebrates creation and the Creator;
is filled with evocative symbols of our past and
    our future;
is firmly placed in the present;
recognizes our failure in responding to God's
    immense love;
is the celebration of the times we encounter God
    during the rest of the week;
is a reminder to be aware of God in our lives;
is a reminder of the Holy Spirit within us

and the world;
is firmly connected with life;
celebrates our bodiliness with gestures and
movements;
is the telling of old stories;
is the telling of new stories;
recognizes and honors our physical nature;
is a time of public prayer for ourselves and the
world;
is the presentation of the gifts of ourselves;
is a resting place in our journey;
is a rejuvenating time;
is a reminder of our baptismal vows;
is a celebration of music, of singing and dancing;
is thanksgiving;
celebrates our sensuality: smelling, tasting,
hearing, speaking/singing, seeing, touching;
is an opportunity to be encouraged by others;
is a banquet;
celebrates the "now" of eternity;
is an opportunity to encourage our companion
travelers by the gift of our presence;
leads us on with renewed enthusiasm in
developing the divine love within all peoples;
is the celebration of life, love, liberty and faith in
Christ through the Holy Spirit;
reflects the radical mutuality that announces the
reign of God;
unites our relationship with God to all of our
other relationships;
is a reminder to recognize the assembled
community as the Body of Christ;
is the Holy Spirit commissioning us as missionaries;

is a sending-forth to help bring about the reign of
   God in the world;
is the ultimate celebration;
is the work of the people.

CONSIDER:

♦ How do I define or describe the liturgy?
   What do I put into the liturgy? What do I get out of
   the liturgy?

♦ How do I go about doing *my* work of the liturgy?

A Celebration of Love

We don't know a lot about the apostles Christ
chose as his followers, for no one at the time
wrote detailed biographies about them.
While some were martyred for their faith, John, the
beloved disciple, was not; John is believed to have
lived to an advanced age.

According to legend, the elderly John was carried
from place to place to preach to the developing
Christian communities. How easy to imagine the
excitement of the people: Here was one of the Twelve!
Here was someone who had heard the Master preach,
had lived with Christ, had been present at the
transfiguration, had been with Christ at the agony in

the garden, had stood with Mary at the foot of the cross, had seen the risen Christ, had been present at the coming of the Holy Spirit at Pentecost.

So when the news went out that he was coming to preach, the people gathered together in excited anticipation. The crowd grew quiet. John looked out over the assembled people. Though his body was frail, his eyes blazed in remembrance of all he had seen and heard and done. John extended his arms over the crowd and looked at them.

Finally he spoke: "Love one another. Again I say to you, love one another."

And that, the legend says, was the sum of John's sermon.

CONSIDER:

♦ How do I assess this summary of the gospel? What is included? What is omitted?

♦ What is the value of having such a summary?

♦ How would I summarize Christ's gospel?

A Celebration of Mistakes

Celebrate our mistakes? Really? Why would we consider such a thing? Yet, that is what we did at the Easter Vigil: "O happy fault, O necessary sin of Adam, / which gained for us so great a Redeemer!"

At the time of making a mistake, at the time of choosing the unwise action or uttering the imprudent remark, it is usually quite difficult to rejoice in our error. We are rattled, self-conscious, angry, chagrined. Later, however, on the sunset side of the error, we realize the benefits, insight, perhaps even wisdom, that resulted from our mistake.

Never to err is not to be our goal, for the only way to avoid making mistakes is to do nothing—and often that is the most costly alternative. Our mistakes—embarrassing, time-consuming, upsetting though they be—testify to our willingness to try. Our mistakes keep us humble. They bring us to our knees to admit the presence of God in the universe. They foster interdependence and community; they initiate prayers for the wisdom and guidance of the Holy Spirit.

We learn from our mistakes. The falls that halt us in our race through life become transformed into the times of most progress.

We learn from our mistakes. The inharmonious notes that we hit in life's song convince us of our need for practice and training.

We learn from our mistakes. The wrong choice at the crossroads leads us to new discoveries in our travels.

We learn from our mistakes. The stark, dark colors on our life's canvas outline the pattern and give balance to the painting.

We learn from our mistakes. The wrong answers we give in life's classroom can initiate our most instructive periods of learning.

We learn from our mistakes. The injudicious tack in our sail through life brings us around to unplanned exploration.

We learn from our mistakes. The dead end in life's maze forces a reappraisal of goals and paths.

Whatever poetic symbols or clever metaphors we want to use in describing the life we live, the important point is that we learn from our mistakes.

And how does this learning take place? Through the power of the Holy Spirit! It is in utilizing the gifts of the Holy Spirit within us that we learn.

And if we need one more reason to celebrate our errors, we know that with the passage of time our misadventures usually make the best stories.

CONSIDER:

♦ What is my response to the above quote from the Easter Vigil liturgy?

♦ What mistakes have I made that later proved beneficial? How did I feel at the time of the error? How do I feel about it now?

♦ How do I feel about making mistakes? What do I fear?

♦ How do I react to the mistakes others make?

A Celebration of the Holy Spirit's Gifts

Come, Holy Spirit! How easy to speak—to shout—those words! How eagerly we pray for peace and joy and love. Come, Holy Spirit!

But as we anticipate Pentecost, longing for the peace-bringing gentleness of the Dove, we must also be prepared to receive the Holy Spirit's searing, consuming flames of fire.

For perhaps the Spirit may not bring us peace. Instead, the gift may be the clear-sightedness to see the injustices that prevent peace.

And perhaps the Spirit may not bring us joy. Instead, the gift may be sensitivity to the unhappiness of others.

And perhaps the Spirit may not bring us love. Instead, the gift may be the awareness of how unloved are those around us.

And perhaps the Spirit may not bring us wisdom. Instead, the gift may be awareness of the need to study and learn.

And perhaps the Spirit may not bring us faith. Instead, the gift may be the refining and purifying crucible of doubt.

And perhaps the Spirit may not bring us kindness. Instead, the gift may be to let the unkindnesses of others assure us of the worth of kindness.

And perhaps the Spirit may not bring us understanding. Instead, the gift may be the savoring of the bitter so that we can comprehend its meaning.

Do we really desire the Spirit's presence—if that presence destroys our comfort and complacency? Surely, we think to ourselves, we are not the ones to fight injustice, to preach the gospel, to change the world. Surely not us!

Perhaps we should refrain from seeking the Spirit's presence. Perhaps we should not even pray, for in divine irony, the answer to our prayers may be the realization that we must change.

And so it is, in fearful apprehension, and with great reluctance, that we do murmur: Come, Holy Spirit.

CONSIDER:

♦ What are some instances when my prayers have been answered—in exactly the opposite way in which I expected? What was my reaction? What was the result?

♦ What particular gifts of the Holy Spirit have I received? How do I use them?

♦ What particular gifts of the Holy Spirit do I especially desire? Why?

The Holy Spirit

Come, Beloved!
Come, for you are called to Pentecost!
In all of time there is but one Resurrection,
but the number of Pentecosts is without limit!

Beloved,
I am the breath that proclaimed,
"Let there be light!"
I am the breath that enfleshed the Word.

I am the light of missionary vision;
I am the light of the mystics and of the stars.

I am the fire of the prophets;
I am the fire of miracles and mystery.

Search for me, Beloved, for I surround you.
Pursue me within.
Rely upon me, for I abide in you.
My breath breathes in you;
my light shines in you;
my flame fires virtue in you.
Search for me, for I am always present.

Projects for the Paschal Season

Projects for Families and Individuals

♦ Write down your personal goals for this Paschal Season, this year, the next five years, the next ten years.

♦ Plan your Paschal Season TV-viewing thoughtfully.

♦ Attend liturgy somewhere other than your home parish: a cathedral, Newman Center, retreat house, monastery, shrine, hospital chapel.

♦ Establish a "prayer corner" in your home and use it daily.

♦ Sign up for a class or workshop that would be helpful to you as an employer, employee or professional; as a spouse, parent or single person.

♦ Attend a liturgy which includes the Anointing of the Sick.

♦ Read about the traditional saints, such as Saint Francis or Saint Thérèse, and also about the modern "saints," such as Dorothy Day, Mohandas Gandhi, Albert Schweitzer, Mother Teresa, Archbishop Oscar Romero.

♦ Greet everyone you meet with a smile.

♦ Begin a new observance of the sabbath.

♦ Take up the study of one timely issue: poverty, nuclear energy, world hunger, homelessness.

♦ Perform a work of mercy daily or weekly.

♦ Spend time sharing a talent or hobby with young people.

♦ Periodically ask yourself the question: "What can I personally do to make this Paschal Season more enjoyable and more holy for my family?"

♦ Join (or organize) an intergenerational Bible study group.

♦ Subscribe to and read a Catholic magazine or newspaper.

♦ Write your own personal prayer of thanksgiving to God.

♦ Begin attending a service of the Liturgy of the Hours: Morning or Evening Prayer.

♦ Undertake one project requiring courage.

♦ Refrain from watching TV news, relying instead on radio, magazines and newspapers.

♦ Make a notebook of hope-filled sayings and stories.

♦ Attend a lecture or dialogue on Judeo-Christian relations.

♦ Read religious or inspirational books/articles that are outside your usual fare.

♦ Take a discovery trip to the library or museum, zoo or concert hall.

♦ Undertake one project that recognizes the world as one global village.

♦ Through books and tapes, learn about relaxation techniques and practice ways to relieve stress.

♦ Teach one adult to read.

♦ Greet every person you encounter by saying to yourself, "I behold the Christ in you."

♦ Memorize one Bible verse each day.

♦ Tell your spouse why you're glad you're married; tell your parents/children why you love them; tell your relatives why they are important to you.

♦ Become a storyteller.

♦ Write a complimentary letter to your pastor. Write a thank-you note to a parish committee or staff person. Write a letter to the media in praise of someone or some action.

- Plan a "memory time" with the family, looking at old photographs, slides or mementos.

- Take time daily to be aware of the movement of the Holy Spirit within you.

- Spend a day in your favorite out-of-doors retreat.

- Invite a non-Catholic friend to a liturgy.

- Become involved with youth through scouting, an athletic organization, Big Brothers or Big Sisters, Junior Great Books, Junior Achievement, exchange student programs or the like.

- Write the history of your family for your children.

- Begin the development of a dormant or neglected talent.

- Allow yourself to do something completely spontaneous and enjoyable.

- Undertake the encouragement of one struggling person.

- Spend a day trying to imagine how to function without your sight or without your hearing or with limited mobility.

- Nurture sensitivity to racist, sexist and homophobic remarks and jokes.

♦ Initiate or nurture a relationship with Mary.

♦ Learn about the foster-grandparent programs in your community.

♦ "Waste" time each week alone with your spouse, or with each of your children, or with someone else important to you.

♦ Volunteer to help new immigrants learn English.

♦ Reevaluate your life-style to make the most prudent use of our natural resources. Set up a definite plan to recycle household/workplace disposables.

♦ Join a car pool to get to work; walk or bicycle where you usually drive.

♦ Become a foster parent or grandparent.

♦ Try to ensure that each day the family eats one meal together.

♦ Seek in love and humility reconciliation with a friend or relative.

♦ Study a second language; plan or dream a visit to a country where that language is spoken.

♦ Take the time to fill out tax forms honestly and justly.

♦ Participate enthusiastically in the singing at liturgy.

- Study the philosophy of nonviolence.

- Read one of the documents of the Second Vatican Council.

- Donate all unused clothing and other articles to charitable organizations.

- Join or encourage others to join the Peace Corps, VISTA or a lay missionary organization.

- Reevaluate the justice of what you pay to others: employees, baby-sitters, and so on.

- Research the causes of one type of pollution.

- Attend or participate in an ethnic festival.

- Spend a specific amount of time in prayer each day.

- Study one group of people that is often a target for prejudice.

- Work toward universal peace by bringing peace with you wherever you go.

- Fast, and donate the money you save to help the needy.

- Sincerely compliment at least one person each day.

- Learn the facts concerning animal and wildlife

conservation. Share what you learn.

♦ Read the encyclicals and bishops' statements concerning justice and peace.

♦ Take time each day (or week) for family prayer or devotions.

♦ Bake a cake, shovel the walk, cut the grass, run an errand, or baby-sit for a friend in need.

♦ Take a serious and honest look at the value system you are giving your children by your example.

♦ Hug each member of your family every day.

♦ Read of the history and customs of the land(s) of your origin.

♦ Evaluate how you do your job with regard to justice to your employer, employees and coworkers.

♦ Pray for peace each day.

♦ Encourage the young to study abroad.

♦ Read the preamble of the charter of the United Nations; if possible, visit the UN.

♦ Join a prayer group, a Scripture-study group, a peace and justice organization.

♦ Hold hands while saying grace at the table.

♦ Attend daily parish worship services as often as possible.

♦ Befriend the children of a single parent.

♦ Write a letter to God each day; afterward sit quietly and listen for an answer.

♦ With the family, research and discuss the customs and history of the Paschal Season.

♦ Take the time to teach your child (grandchild, neighbor's child) one specific thing—an activity, hobby, aspect of nature.

♦ Daily entrust to God the loved one about whom you are most concerned.

♦ Once a week discuss with your family a movie or TV program.

♦ Visit the Holy Land in person or via books and films from your library.

♦ Practice seeing the humorous side of every difficult situation.

♦ Have a home-blessing ceremony with your family.

♦ Take the family on a special outing that interests everyone.

♦ Share your heritage with your children,

grandchildren, nieces, nephews or young friends.

♦ Practice daily being aware of the presence of God.

♦ Listen to a recording or attend a performance of
  Jesus Christ Superstar, Godspell or some other such
  musical with your family. Discuss with them
  afterward this interpretation of Christ's life.

♦ Use a Christ Candle at family meals.

♦ Begin to tithe: Give ten percent of all your income to
  God through the Church or other charities
  according to the biblical custom.

♦ Pray with your coworkers.

♦ Request a favor from someone who usually has little
  to give.

♦ Determine each day, upon rising, that you shall be
  joyful. Your first prayer of the day might be: "This is
  the day that the LORD has made; let us be glad and
  rejoice in it" (Psalm 118:24).

♦ Spend time each day in spiritual reading.

♦ Answer each phone call in a friendly and happy
  manner.

♦ Tell your spouse/children/family daily of your love.

♦ Confront your greatest worry or fear, turning the

matter over to God each day.

♦ Offer to your friends and neighbors rides to church.

♦ Begin taking music (or art or drama or dance) lessons.

♦ Compile a notebook of items of joy—uplifting thoughts, pleasant memories, things that make you smile, reminders of God's goodness to you and the wonderment of life.

♦ Volunteer at a battered women's shelter, a hospital, a shelter for the homeless, a hospice, a prison.

♦ Join a clown ministry.

♦ Make a list of all the right choices you have made in your life—and thank the Holy Spirit!

♦ Sing! Include at least one song of praise in your daily prayers.

♦ Save the cartoons, jokes and day-brighteners from newspapers and magazines to include with letters.

♦ Take a friend to your favorite wilderness or nature spot, to the zoo or the botanical gardens.

♦ Make a retreat or a Marriage Encounter/Engaged Encounter weekend.

♦ Send a complimentary letter to a politician or

government employee.

♦ Teach a child a game or song or nursery rhyme.

♦ Write a thank-you letter to someone who was important to you in your youth.

♦ Plant a garden.

♦ Give a special gift to a favorite child.

♦ Include a hymn or song in your family prayers.

♦ Donate blood to a blood bank.

♦ Do something "silly" for someone you love.

♦ Support the establishment in your neighborhood of a residential home for the retarded or mentally ill, or a halfway home for the chemically dependent or for former prisoners.

♦ Take a CPR (Cardiopulmonary Resuscitation) course.

♦ Develop the habit of smiling at those anonymous people who serve your needs—traffic officers, store clerks, bus drivers, custodians.

♦ Attend a Special Olympics event.

♦ Host a surprise party for someone you love—with no other reason for the party except your love.

◆ Extend to others your unique life experiences—as the parent of a handicapped child, the spouse of one afflicted with an incurable illness, the relative of someone who committed suicide, etc.

◆ Assist refugees and immigrants in finding homes and jobs.

◆ Take a "joy" break each day.

◆ Do one specific thing to help create a Christian environment at your job or place of business.

◆ Become involved in a parish activity that ministers to others.

◆ In a specific way, register your objection against the prevalence of violence and sex on television.

◆ Become involved in politics.

◆ Befriend a "street person."

◆ Make a list of the various symbols of the season you encounter each day and discuss them with your family.

◆ Spend some time with the aged, widowed, homebound.

◆ Work for legislation protecting the vulnerable, such as the newborn and the criminally insane.

- Support a child or an aged person in a foreign country through a monthly contribution to a foundation or organization.

- Share a special talent or interest with the young or the disadvantaged.

- Become involved in the RCIA (Rite of Christian Initiation of Adults) program.

- Take time to watch the sunrise.

- Compile a list of all the people who have been important to you and why.

- Pray daily for people who cannot worship freely.

- Write a "Thank-you-for-being-you" letter to a friend.

- Take to a concert or theater or museum someone who ordinarily would not be able to attend.

- Teach a parish religion class.

- Contribute money or time to an organization for the handicapped.

- Spend time with an older person.

- Do something special for those who work with youth.

- Contribute to the symphony, theater or museum.

♦ Volunteer with the local food pantry or meal-serving program.

♦ While writing letters or cards, pray for each person or family.

♦ Make a list of the gifts you take for granted: life, sight, freedom, mobility, opportunity.

♦ Read the assigned Scriptures for each day.

♦ Write a story or poem about the Paschal Mystery.

♦ On an especially hectic day, take time to reflect on the meaning of the Paschal Season.

♦ Have an Easter party.

♦ Tape record the memories of the oldest members of the family.

♦ Write a letter to a person who has inspired you.

♦ Rewrite the Our Father in your own words.

♦ Adopt, anonymously, a needy family, by giving gifts, sending notes of encouragement and praying.

♦ Choose a new family tradition for this year.

♦ Give up a favorite grudge.

♦ Sing or recite all the verses of an appropriate Lent,

Easter or Pentecost hymn or song as part of family prayer or as a table grace.

♦ Introduce a family discussion on the sacredness of everyday life.

♦ When encountering impolite or rude people, pause and say a prayer for them, blessing them in their time of impatience.

♦ Compose a creed of your beliefs.

♦ Make your own Paschal Season record book to keep. Include journal entries, pictures from magazines and newspapers, quotes from cards or hymns, names of visitors, moments of inspiration, memorable events, Scripture texts, etc. (This can also be a family project with all ages contributing.)

♦ Fast or abstain during Eastertide in joyful anticipation of Pentecost.

♦ Bless your children, your parents, your spouse, your other relatives, your friends, your coworkers, the ill and dying.

♦ Choose one or more ways to celebrate in a special way the Easter Season: the time from Easter to Pentecost.

♦ Research Lenten customs and Easter Season projects of different ethnic groups, and especially those of your own heritage.

♦ Increase children's awareness of the poor and needy by helping them contribute to an appropriate organization.

♦ Have a Scripture cake-baking party. Use this recipe from *A Continual Feast*, by Evelyn Birge Vitz:

Scripture Cake

> *The recipe for Scripture Cake was often set up as a puzzle or exercise and its underlying goal was to make you look up the reference, read the Bible.... I have set it up here so that the answers are given.*

1 1/2 cups (3 sticks) Psalms 55:21 (butter)
2 cups Jeremiah 6:20 (sugar)
6 Jeremiah 17:11 (eggs)
1/2 cup Judges 4:19 (milk)
2 tablespoons 1 Samuel 14:25 (honey)
4 1/2 cups Leviticus 6:15 (flour)
A pinch of Leviticus 2:13 (salt)
2 tablespoons Amos 4:5 (baking powder)
2 Chronicles 9:9 (spices: 1 teaspoon cinnamon
   and 1/2 teaspoon freshly ground nutmeg)
2 cups 1 Samuel 30:12 (raisins)
2 cups Numbers 13:23 (figs), chopped
1 cup Numbers 17:8 (almonds), chopped or
   grated

Many recipes for Scripture Cake add to this list of ingredients only the words: "Follow Solomon's recipe for making a good boy and you will have a good cake, Proverbs 23:14"—"Beat well." I think I'll be a little more specific!

Preheat the oven to 350° F. Butter and flour loaf pans, small or large disposable aluminum pans, or a bundt or tube pan.

In a large bowl, cream the butter until light

and creamy. Beat in the sugar until fluffy. Add
the eggs one at a time, beating well after each
addition. Stir in the milk and the honey.
Sift the flour with the salt, baking powder,
and dry spices.
Add the dry ingredients gradually to the wet.
Mix only until thoroughly blended. Stir in the
raisins, figs, and almonds.
Turn the mixture into the pans.
Bake for about 50 minutes, or until a straw
inserted in the center comes out clean.
Yield: 1 large or several small cakes
Variation: You can halve this recipe if you
like.

♦ Make a list of your blessings!

♦ Begin a prayer-record: List petitions and dates for
later reference.

♦ Visit an "empty" church.

FOR LENT:

♦ Attend Ash Wednesday services.

♦ Do one good deed each day—anonymously!

♦ Admit your problem and join the appropriate
Twelve-Step program: Alcoholics Anonymous, Al-
Anon, Overeaters Anonymous, Emotions
Anonymous, Sexaholics Anonymous, Gamblers
Anonymous or whatever.

- Come face-to-face with your deepest fear and make a definite plan to deal with it.

- Make a cross.

- Sign a donor card directing that any usable organs be designated for transplant on your death. Discuss this with those close to you.

- Write a letter of support and encouragement to a catechumen or candidate preparing to come into the Church at the Easter Vigil.

- Give a treasured item to a loved one, explaining why the item is meaningful to you.

- Attend ecumenical Lenten services.

- Turn over your "hopeless" situation to God each day.

- Make a list of all the things that you do with your body and senses in the course of one day.

- Recall one person who was instrumental in your early formation. Choose one specific way you can pass on to another the gift that person gave to you.

- To deepen your understanding of the Last Supper, celebrate a Passover meal with your family.

- Volunteer at a hospice.

♦ Make Easter baskets for your friends, including adults.

♦ Make Easter decorations for the house.

♦ Send Easter cards to people with whom you usually do not correspond—especially someone who is lonely, widowed, homebound, or grieving the recent death of a loved one.

♦ Make a daily examination of conscience.

♦ Seek out a spiritual adviser.

♦ Learn about the healing of memories, and pray daily for the healing of life's hurts and for forgiveness of others.

♦ Abstain from meat or some other specific food or drink, with no purpose other than to remind yourself of God's love and mercy.

♦ Make out your will.

♦ Pray each day for the dead, especially those who have touched your life.

♦ Volunteer to help other people from your church serve food after funerals.

♦ Do one difficult task each day.

♦ Choose the readings and music for your funeral.

◆ Do a specific act of love to someone seemingly unlovable.

◆ Examine your attachment to the things of this world as you daily recycle or give away at least one item.

◆ Abstain on a daily or even hourly basis from one specific bad habit—such as gossiping, wasting time, being messy, procrastinating.

◆ If you are involved in a Twelve-Step program, make a fifth step.

◆ Pray each day for the acceptance of your cross.

◆ Visit a funeral home and discuss the arrangements for your funeral.

◆ Frequent the Sacrament of Reconciliation, especially communal services.

◆ Pray each day for self-forgiveness and the release from regrets.

◆ Abstain from coffee breaks and donate the money to a special cause.

◆ Write love letters to be opened only after your death to people who are important to you.

◆ Abstain from watching television or listening to the stereo.

♦ Pray daily for that difficult person in your life.

♦ Fast from one half hour of sleep and spend the time in prayer.

♦ Choose an epitaph for your tombstone.

♦ List what you would do if you knew you had only one year (or one month) to live.

♦ Fast in reparation for your sins of commission and omission.

♦ Make a list of the legacies—not goods or money, but attitudes, standards of value and influences—that you are passing on to your survivors.

♦ Share with your family a time of family reconciliation.

♦ Pray the Stations of the Cross daily or weekly.

♦ Choose a new tradition to do as an individual during this Lenten Season.

♦ Pray the rosary, meditating on the sorrowful mysteries.

♦ Decorate your home for Lent.

♦ Fast or abstain in joyful anticipation of the Resurrection and for those to be received into the

Church at the Easter Vigil.

♦ Attend Triduum services.

♦ Plant a tree.

♦ Decorate for Easter.

♦ Include Easter hymns as part of your family devotions.

♦ Make your own Easter cards.

♦ Decorate a tree or bush with Easter eggs or other decorations.

♦ Show love in a special way to someone every day.

♦ Celebrate one or more Easter traditions with your family.

♦ Surprise each member of your family with an Easter gift.

♦ Use an Easter or Christ candle on the dinner table.

♦ Write a thank-you note to the pastor, choir director or others who helped make the Lent/Triduum services especially meaningful.

♦ Write a congratulations and welcome note to someone baptized and/or confirmed on Holy Saturday.

♦ Pray to the Holy Spirit daily.

♦ Use the water blessed at the Easter Vigil to bless your home, family, guests and Easter dinner.

♦ Discuss with your family the traditions and symbols of Easter.

♦ Give Easter gifts to some of your friends in place of Christmas presents.

♦ Plant a garden, sharing the experience of gardening with a young person and the produce of the garden with a friend.

♦ Make a May altar in honor of Mary in your home.

♦ Celebrate with your family the feast of Ascension, possibly using balloons and kites.

♦ Attend Evensong or Vespers with a friend on Pentecost.

♦ Use decorations of red on the feast of Pentecost.

♦ Discuss with your family the symbols for Pentecost.

♦ Listen with your family to a recording of *The*

Messiah or attend a performance of it.

♦ Attend daily liturgy as often as possible.

♦ Pray the rosary during Eastertide, meditating on the glorious mysteries.

♦ Make a list of all the things that you do with your body and senses in the course of one day.

♦ During family time together, read aloud the Easter cards you received.

Projects for Groups and Organizations

♦ Undertake one project to beautify the world.

♦ Make a special effort to welcome immigrants to your church and community.

♦ Undertake one community conservation or recycling project.

♦ Join with others in evaluating waste at home and at work.

♦ Undertake one project with youth.

♦ Research ways in which the surpluses and shortages in the world can be reconciled.

♦ Undertake one project in the cause of human rights.

♦ Make a booklet of Paschal Season memories, poems, meditations and artwork contributed by members. Copies of this booklet could be gifts to the members, the parish or organization.

♦ Plan a visit to a nursing home, hospital or senior center to sing, entertain or just talk with the residents.

♦ Plan an activity to help others prepare for Easter, such as take an elderly or handicapped person shopping, decorate a nursing home.

♦ Adopt, anonymously, a needy family, by giving gifts, sending notes of encouragement and praying.

♦ Get involved in a project to help the homeless or needy during this season.

♦ Choose a project to help bring about the Kingdom of God, such as a social justice concern.

Prayers for the Paschal Season

Introduction

We Christians have been instructed, commanded, urged and begged to "pray always!" To make our faithfulness to prayer easier, we have been graced with variety in prayer: spontaneous prayer, meditative prayer, formal prayer.

In spontaneous prayer we use our own words and thoughts; spontaneous prayer is influenced by the moment and by being our personal prayer.

Meditative prayer is the quiet opening up of ourselves to the voice of God and the presence of the Holy Spirit within us.

Formal prayer uses words—and sometimes gestures, ritual and music—composed by others. The eucharistic liturgy is formal prayer; so too, Liturgy of the Hours, the rosary, novenas, and the familiar traditional prayers.

All three types of prayer are important. Lent and Eastertide, by drawing our attention to the necessity of prayer, encourage us to improve our prayer life.

A few suggestions:

♦ Set aside time each day for prayer.

♦ Choose a psalm to read each day during Lent or Eastertide.

♦ Choose a prayer to say each day during Lent or Eastertide. (Some possibilities follow.)

New Seasonal Prayers

A PRAYER FOR THE WORLD

O Trinity of Love,
    first and most perfect community of persons,
In your love and generosity
    you have given us an entire universe for our
    home.

Rid us of our greed so that there will be enough for
    all.
Open our hearts to trust one another lest,
    in our mutual fear, we perish.
Make us intolerant of prejudice of every kind,
    for we are all your children,
    created to live in harmony and peace.
Make us sensitive to the needs of others.
Help us to hear the cries of those who have no
    voice: the poor, the weak, the enslaved.
Make us see that our enemies are poverty and
    disease and ignorance,
        not our brothers and sisters.
Fill us with the imagination and determination
    to solve the many problems of this war-scarred
    world.
Direct us to the solutions that those who don't know
    you say don't exist.
Grant that our love of justice and desire for peace
    can transcend the bounds of selfishness and
    suspicion, arrogance and apathy.

We come to you, O Blessed Trinity,
  for you can inspire us in our endeavors.
Give us courage and renew our failing spirits.
We ask your help
  so that all you have created, saved and sanctified
  may be brought to the fullness of love which you,
  even more than we, desire.
Within your love is our hope.
Within your love is our peace, both now and
  evermore. Amen.

A TRINITARIAN PRAYER FOR HOPE

O God of Creation,
you direct the migrating butterflies
  and awaken the hibernating raccoons;
you change tadpoles into frogs
  and crawling creatures into flying ones;
you design the movement of stars and planets and
  galaxies;
  and you have created the mystery that is me.

Give me hope—
hope that guides me when I am traveling through
  days that seem without purpose;
hope that sustains me
  when I must wait for the world, others, you;
hope that confers courage
  when I am afraid to grow;
hope that comforts me
  when I am confused by the vast mysteries of life.

O God of Salvation,
you responded to the sick and suffering,
    the sinful, the lonely and the lowly;
you offered yourself to us
    as our Way, our Truth, our Life;
you thought of others
    even in your final agony.

Give me hope—
hope that soothes me
    through times of suffering and depression,
    pain and loneliness;
hope that guides me
    during my wanderings and quests;
hope that bears me up
    through loss and bereavement
    and the anticipation of my own death.

O God of Sanctification,
you counseled the prophets of old
    and the writers of the holy books;
you transformed those timid disciples
    into brave proclaimers of the Word;
you inspired the saints,
    both the celebrated and the unknown.

Give me hope—
hope that replaces doubt with wisdom and
    understanding;
hope that heals the pain of insecurity;
hope that allows me no choice but to persevere.

Make me bold, O God, in my hope.
Help me to see beyond the limits that,
    in my trepidation, I have set for myself.

Help me to see beyond the limits that,
  in my audacity, I have set for you.
I ask these things, O Divine Trinity,
  because I believe in you
  who are my hope of glory everlasting. Amen.

A PRAYER FOR JOY

O God of marvel and mystery, make me joyous!
Bless me with the healing and forgiving power of
  laughter.
Help me to delight in life's wonderment and
  surprises.
Preserve me from sanctimonious solemnity and
  morose morality,
  and deliver me from the vanity of regrets.
Remove from me the perverse tendency
  to make mountains out of the molehills of my life.
Help me to regard the duck's waddle,
  the monkey's antics
  and my own foibles with the same sense of
  humor.
Remind me that I am important,
  not for what I do but for what I am—
  your child, created in your image.
Help me to realize
  that it is your love that gives meaning to my
    existence,
  and that joy and laughter and singing
  are echoes to that tremendous love.
Let me not forget to be joyful!

Let me not be too hurried to be cheerful.
Let me not be too busy to smile.
I ask these things, my Lord and my God, so that
someday I may join with all the mirthful saints
and singing angels
in praising you eternally. Amen.

A PRAYER FOR PENTECOST

Inflame me, O Trinity of love, with fervor!
Quicken within me, my Creator, the life of your
grace.
Make me yearn, my Savior and Teacher,
to carry out your gospel of love.
Spirit of Pentecost, consume me with the fire of
action.

Help me to proclaim your divine word
in thought and spirit and deed.
Help me to realize that by my Baptism
I have been called to your priesthood
and to be a witness to you, who live within me.
Help me to recognize opportunities to show love.
Make me brave enough to stretch out my hand
to those in need.
Let me share my story with those in trauma—
even if the cost is renewed pain from old wounds.
Give me the creative courage to undertake tasks
never before accomplished
and the inspired wisdom and determination
to complete them.

Come into my heart,
   to bestow upon me your many gifts.
Change my fear to boldness,
   my reticence to ardor,
   my concern for self to concern for others.
I ask these things, O my God,
   so that through my faithfulness to you
   others may come to know and love you,
   who are the source of all love. Amen.

PRAYER TO LADY WISDOM (See Wisdom 7:7-12)

Dear Lady Wisdom,
be with us today as we search for who we are
   and who you are.
Guide and inspire our thoughts and words;
   let them overflow with the creativity and laughter
   that you bring to our world.
Protect us from the paths of pride and self-
   righteousness.
Teach us to dance and sing in your beauty and
   freedom.
Help us to grow in wisdom and grace, love and joy.
Amen.

With complete confidence we approach you, God, with our petitions. You have assured us that no prayer is unheeded, for your blessings are ever available to the poor in spirit, the suffering, the needy. You have given to us the gift of community, but we are not always open to your gifts. And so we ask your help, God, that we may respond to your call.

In the presence of the poor,
we ask forgiveness for our extravagance, our dehumanizing charity, our complacency with the cycle of poverty. Hear us, God of all.

In the presence of the hungry,
we ask forgiveness for our greed, our wastefulness, our talking, talking, talking.
Hear us, God of all.

In the presence of the oppressed,
we ask forgiveness for our apathy to injustice, our forgetfulness of their suffering, our contentment with studying the problem. Hear us, God of all.

In the presence of the weary,
we ask forgiveness for our insensitivity to their burdens, our unopened hands, our self-indulgent strength. Hear us, God of all.

In the presence of the sorrowing,
we ask forgiveness for our callousness, our neglect, our distance. Hear us, God of all.

In the presence of living saints,

we ask forgiveness for doubting them, for
doubting miracles, for doubting you, O God.
Hear us, God of all.

In the presence of the homeless,
we ask forgiveness for our closed-door
hospitality, our certitude of stereotypes, the
self-righteousness of our comfortable nights.
Hear us, God of all.

In the presence of the handicapped,
we ask forgiveness for our ignorance, our barbed
laughter, our pride in our wholeness. Hear us,
God of all.

In the presence of the gentle,
we ask forgiveness for the clamor of our
arrogance, our violence, our disregard of their
value. Hear us, God of all.

In the presence of the lonely,
we ask forgiveness for our over-commitment, our
self-absorption, our convenient diversions. Hear
us, God of all.

In the presence of the vulnerable,
we ask forgiveness for our failure to recognize
their humanity, our failure to uphold their
dignity, our failure to protect their lives. Hear us,
God of all.

In the presence of justice-seekers,
we ask forgiveness for our inaudible support, our
fear of innovative solutions, our preoccupation
with our own security. Hear us, God of all.

In the presence of the unemployed,
we ask forgiveness for our superior attitude, our

prejudices, our platitudes. Hear us, God of all.

In the presence of the persecuted,
we ask forgiveness for our silence, our fear of
appearing radical, our convenient denial of
atrocities. Hear us, God of all.

In the presence of our enemies,
we ask forgiveness for our merciless legalism,
our creative rationalizations, our reluctance to
forgive. Hear us, God of all.

In the presence of strangers,
we ask forgiveness for our hostilities, our
imaginative evasions, our failure to recognize
Christ in them. Hear us, God of all.

In the presence of the suffering,
we ask forgiveness for the scarcity of our tears,
our impatience with their pain, our Band Aid help
for their gaping wounds. Hear us, God of all.

In the presence of the peacemakers,
we ask forgiveness for our wise cynicism, our
alibis for noninvolvement, our contributing
toward world annihilation. Hear us, God of all.

In the presence of our friends,
we ask forgiveness for our failure to appreciate
them, our failure to cheer them, our failure to
inspire them. Hear us, God of all.

In the presence of our families,
we ask forgiveness for our thoughtlessness, our
lack of time for them, our reluctance to express
our love. Hear us, God of all.

In the presence of you, our God,
we ask forgiveness for our misuse of your gifts,

our unquestioning faith in our own abilities, our hoarding of your limitless love. Hear us, God of all.

You have chosen us to be the channels of your divine love. Help us to heed your call, for in serving others, we praise, honor and serve you. We offer these petitions in the name of the Trinity—the Creator, the Savior, the Sanctifier. Amen.

PRAYER TO THE HOLY SPIRIT

Spirit most holy, come!
Quiet the clamor around me
so I can hear the sounds of your presence.
Silence the selfishness within me
so I can hear your whispers of wisdom.

Spirit most holy, come!
You have chosen me—
in spite of my fears—
as an instrument of divine love.
You have chosen me—
in spite of my inadequacies—
to speak your wisdom to others.
You have chosen me—
in spite of my reluctance—
to touch others with your compassion.

What incredible faith, O God,
you have in me!
Spirit most holy, come!

PRAYER TO THE HOLY SPIRIT
(Based on Romans 5:1-5 and 8:1-22)

Spirit most holy!
Splendid Divinity,
Sanctifying Stillness,
Sustaining Breath,
you dwell in all who live in Christ.
As you were present at Christ's rising,
so you are present with us now.

Spirit most holy!
Give us life that we may pray,
for without you, we cannot.
Yet with you, through you,
we declare ourselves followers of Christ.
With you, through you,
we dare to claim our inheritance with Christ.
With you, through you,
in triumphant certitude,
in radical intimacy,
we call God "our Father"!
Teach us to pray!

Spirit most holy!
Give us life that we may have faith—
faith made holy by your presence
and by our actions,
faith firmly rooted in the sphere of your grace,
a faith extending far beyond
all that we can do.
Give us faith!

Spirit most holy!
Give us life that we may be free—
free from the terrors that paralyze us,
free from our bonds of death:
    death from sin,
    death from fear,
    death from suffering,
    death from your enmity.
Replace these disabling bonds!
Free us with the living, searing fire
    of commitment to Christ,
through you.

Spirit most holy!
Give us life that we may have vision—
vision to see beyond today,
beyond suffering and disappointment
and the powers of present pain.
Fill our hearts and minds and thoughts
with eager longing
for the glory that is to be.
Give us vision!

Spirit most holy!
Give us life that we may have your guidance—
guidance that sustains us
during these days which are upon us.
As we are united forever in Christ's love
be our companion now
and our driving force
during the times that are to come.

Spirit most holy!
With you is peace—
the peace of Christ,
the peace of God.
And so, Spirit of Life,
we your children,
join with all creation,
in exclaiming,
come, Holy Spirit, come!

Traditional Prayers

PRAYER OF SAINT FRANCIS OF ASSISI

Lord, make me an instrument of your peace:
where there is hatred, let me sow love;
where there is injury, pardon;
where there is doubt, faith;
where there is despair, hope;
where there is darkness, light;
and where there is sadness, joy.

O Divine Master,
grant that I may not so much seek
to be consoled as to console;
to be understood as to understand;
to be loved as to love.

For it is in giving that we receive;
it is in pardoning that we are pardoned;
and it is in dying that we are born to eternal life.

THE CANTICLE OF BROTHER SUN

Most High, all-powerful, good Lord,
    Yours are the praises, the glory, the honor, and
        all blessing.
To you alone, Most High, they belong,
    and no one is worthy to mention your name.

Praised be you, my Lord, with all your creatures,

especially Sir Brother Sun,
who is the day and through whom you give us
light.
And he is beautiful and radiant with great
splendor,
and bears a likeness of you, Most High One.

Praised be you, my Lord, through Sister Moon and
the stars;
in heaven you formed them clear and precious
and beautiful.

Praised be you, my Lord, through Brother Wind,
and through the air, cloudy and serene,
and every kind of weather
through which you give sustenance to your
creatures.

Praised be you, my Lord, through Sister Water,
which is very useful and humble and precious and
chaste.

Praised be you, my Lord, through Brother Fire,
through whom you light the night,
and he is beautiful and playful and robust and
strong.

Praised be you, my Lord, through our Sister Mother
Earth,
who sustains and governs us,
and who produces varied fruits with colored
flowers and herbs.

Praised be you, my Lord,
through those who give pardon for your love
and bear infirmity and tribulation.

Blessed are those who endure in peace,
  for by yo Most High, they shall be crowned.

Praised be you, my Lord, through our Sister Bodily
    Death,
  from whom no living person can escape.
Woe to those who die in mortal sin.
Blessed are those whom death will find in your most
    holy will,
  for the second death shall do them no harm.
Praise and bless my Lord and give him thanks
  and serve him with great humility.

PRAYER OF THE CHRISTOPHERS

I am only one, Lord, but I am one.
I cannot do everything, but I can do something.
What I can do, I ought to do.
And what I ought to do, by your grace, I will do.
Amen.

THE SORROWFUL MYSTERIES OF THE ROSARY

1. The Agony in the Garden
2. The Scourging
3. The Crowning With Thorns
4. The Carrying of the Cross
5. The Crucifixion

THE GLORIOUS MYSTERIES OF THE ROSARY

1. The Resurrection
2. The Ascension
3. The Descent of the Holy Spirit
4. The Assumption of Mary
5. The Crowning of Mary as Queen of Heaven

BLESSING OF AARON

The LORD bless you and keep you;
the LORD make his face to shine upon you, and
  be gracious to you;
the LORD lift up his countenance upon you, and
  give you peace.
(Numbers 6:24-26)

STATIONS OF THE CROSS

1. Jesus Is Condemned to Death
2. Jesus Accepts His Cross
3. Jesus Falls the First Time
4. Jesus Meets His Mother
5. Simon Helps Jesus Carry His Cross
6. Veronica Wipes Jesus' Face
7. Jesus Falls the Second Time
8. Jesus Speaks to the Weeping Women
9. Jesus Falls the Third Time
10. Jesus Is Stripped of His Garments
11. Jesus Is Nailed to the Cross
12. Jesus Dies on the Cross

13. Jesus Is Taken Down From the Cross
14. Jesus Is Laid in the Tomb
Many people add a Fifteenth Station: Jesus Is Risen!

PRAYER FOR A HAPPY DEATH

Jesus, Mary and Joseph, I give you my heart and
soul.
Jesus, Mary and Joseph, assist me in my last agony.
Jesus, Mary and Joseph, may I breathe forth my
soul in peace with you.

SOUL OF CHRIST

Soul of Christ, sanctify me.
Body of Christ, save me.
Blood of Christ, inebriate me.
Water from the side of Christ, wash me.
Passion of Christ, strengthen me.
O good Jesus, hear me.
Within your wounds hide me.
Separated from you let me never be.
From the malignant enemy defend me.
At the hour of death, call me.
To come to you, bid me,
that I may praise you in the company
of your saints for all eternity. Amen.

PRAYER TO JESUS CRUCIFIED

Look down upon me, good and gentle Jesus, while before your face I humbly kneel, and with burning soul pray and beseech you to fix deep in my heart lively sentiments of faith, hope and charity, true contrition for my sins, and a firm purpose of amendment, while I contemplate with great love and tender pity your five wounds, pondering over them within me, calling to mind the words which David, your prophet, said of you, my good Jesus: "They have pierced my hands and my feet; they have numbered all my bones."

ACT OF CONTRITION

O my God, I am heartily sorry for having offended you, and I detest all my sins because of your just punishments, but most of all because they offend you, my God, who are all good and deserving of all love. I firmly resolve, with the help of your grace, to sin no more and to avoid the occasions of sin. Amen.

SEQUENCE FROM THE FEAST OF PENTECOST

Come, Holy Spirit, come!
And from your celestial home
Shed a ray of light divine!

Come, Father of the poor!

Come, source of all our store!
Come, within our bosoms shine!

You, of comforters the best;
You, the soul's most welcome guest;
Sweet refreshment here below;

In our labor, rest most sweet;
Grateful coolness in the heat;
Solace in the midst of woe.

O most blessed Light divine,
Shine within these hearts of yours,
And our inmost being fill!

Where you are not, we have naught,
Nothing good in deed or thought,
Nothing free from taint of ill.

Heal our wounds, our strength renew;
On our dryness, pour your dew;
Wash the stains of guilt away.

Bend the stubborn heart and will;
Melt the frozen, warm the chill;
Guide the steps that go astray.

On the faithful, who adore
And confess you, evermore
In your sev'nfold gift descend;

Give them virtue's sure reward;
Give them your salvation, Lord;
Give them joys that never end. Amen. Alleluia.